Notes

on the

Kitchen Table

❧

To Lynda –
Leave a note !
[signature] *– 98 –*

NOTES

on the

KITCHEN TABLE

℘

Families Offer Messages
of Hope
for Generations to Come

Bob Greene & D. G. Fulford

DOUBLEDAY

New York   Toronto   London
Sydney   Auckland

PUBLISHED BY DOUBLEDAY
a division of Bantam Doubleday Dell Publishing Group, Inc.
1540 Broadway, New York, New York 10036

DOUBLEDAY and the portrayal of an anchor with a dolphin
are trademarks of Doubleday, a division of
Bantam Doubleday Dell Publishing Group, Inc.

Library of Congress Cataloging-in-Publication Data
Notes on the kitchen table : families offer messages of hope for
generations to come / [edited by] Bob Greene and
D. G. Fulford. — 1st ed.
p.   cm.
1. Conduct of life—Quotations, maxims, etc.   2. Maxims, American.
I. Greene, Bob.   II. Fulford, D. G.
BJ1581.2.N67   1998
081—dc21   97-44309
CIP

ISBN: 0-385-49061-5

Book Design by Lynne Amft

*For Maggie, Amanda, Nick,
Tucker, and Hannah*

Contents

Notes

on the

Kitchen Table

∾

F i r s t l y

The voices that come from the hearts of families can be wondrous.

When we wrote *To Our Children's Children,* our intention was a simple one. The book was a collection of over one thousand questions, meant to be small, precise and evocative, offering readers a way to tell family stories through the pleasurable act of remembering.

The idea behind the book was that recording a personal history can be as easy as writing a letter. With the questions in the book providing a starting point, we wanted families to sit down and tell the stories of their own lives—to pass down those stories to generations to come. Hundreds of thousands of families have done just that—have used the book to pass along family treasures made of words.

At the end of the book, we asked an additional question:

If you had to write a note—one note—and leave it propped against the sugar bowl on your kitchen table for future generations to read, what would you say in that note?

Families took the time to answer that question, and put those answers in the mail to us. Notes arrived on engraved stationery, on lined notebook paper, on cards decorated with flowers and pictures of kittens. Some were typed, some were handwritten, some were sent by sons or granddaughters or in-laws.

Some were written in classes held at senior centers or continuing education facilities.

Some were written in bed.

Some at the kitchen table.

These notes came from all over the country and straight from the senders' hearts; from men and women to children they love and to grandchildren not yet born. These were echoes consciously preserved, meant to sound anew in the future. They were messages from a world of hope, of kept promises and back screen doors.

People of all generations took the time to record the importance of kindness and hard work, of spiritual belief and respect for nature, of honesty and integrity and lifelong learning. They praised risk-taking and acknowledged adversity and imperfection. They spoke of a need for tolerance and forgiveness, both for oneself and for others. They quoted their own parents and grandparents; they quoted George Washington Carver and William Blake.

They gave of themselves, to their children and to their children's children—and to all of us. They provided abundant evidence of the enduring strength of family love, both for those lucky enough to have it, and for those aspiring to build such a foundation themselves.

This book is the result of their notes on the kitchen table. The words of the men and women who wrote notes are here, as are brief stories about many of their lives—amplification of the events that have shaped them and their families. We received far too many notes for us to publish all of them in this volume; in addition to the notes we were able to include, we have tried to summarize some of the spirit behind the notes. The messages both said and unsaid.

They are, we have found and truly believe, the values that families live by and wish to pass along.

N o t e s

In the absence of the human voice, there is nothing like the written word: thoughts put down by the hand of someone you love. These are thoughts that can be touched, thoughts that can be discovered down through the years, folded and tucked like treasure inside a drawer.

What a small courtesy a note is, waiting to be found. It speaks simply, yet profoundly, of connection, continuity and caring.

A house is never empty when there is a note waiting on the table. The warmest and most welcoming sight to see when you open the door.

R e q u e s t

This is what we asked:

If you had to write a note—one note—and leave it propped against the sugar bowl on your kitchen table for future generations to read, what would you say in that note?

It might be a bit of philosophy you've learned over the years; it might be a helpful tip or piece of guidance. It might be a thought about the meaning of your life; it might be your most heartfelt wishes for the people who read it. Intimate or humorous, it can be anything you want.

One note—one note to leave in the kitchen, for your children's children, and theirs, and all of ours.

Foreword

If you should be the one to read,
This note upon the table,
Come in, sit down, rest awhile,
Slowly sip a cup of coffee or tea,
Or perhaps you prefer a Pepsi,
Relax, think happy thoughts, and smile,
As you ponder here awhile,
Think of your blessings,
Counting them one by one,
And, when you are rested, refreshed and able,
Give yourself a hug from me,
Then as you leave, please close the door,
Knowing it was for you especially,
I left this note upon the table.
     Signed with love, from me.
     Bernice Whitlock
     ATALISSA, IOWA

Bernice Whitlock is a farmer's daughter, born in Iowa. She was widowed at age sixty-nine after fifty years of marriage. She remarried seven years after that. She wrote this poem on the day before her seventy-fourth birthday. She has three children and six grandchildren.

Inheritance

To our family's future generations:

This is a letter to my future, from your past. If I could know you, impart some things to you, these would be my thoughts:

I'd want you to know that you were loved, you future generations, even before you were born.

That you were considered in the way our family lives its lives now, in the choices we make and in our attempts to preserve a family history and to keep our extended family strongly connected. We've traced our genealogy to the year 1760 in Syria. How lucky you are to have this recorded history to explore! I hope you will do so with the same sense of discovery and awe that I have felt. Even as I write this, I am picturing how full and beautifully varied our family tree will be as you add your name.

Some say that the world is in decline and that there will be nothing left of the environment or civilized society in the future. For some reason, I've never felt that at all. It's true that much is wrong with the world, but in everything there is hope. Three months ago I had a nearly fatal car accident; today my front yard is an explosion of daffodils and a new baby was born into our family two weeks ago. I'm not afraid for you. God is obviously at work.

Love,
Victoria Louise Tamoush
TUJUNGA, CALIFORNIA

∽

Victoria Tamoush is forty-one and has four nieces and nephews.

"I didn't know if I was going to live," she says. "I started thinking about all these meetings I couldn't attend, all these committees. And I thought about someday quitting them completely, either because I was too tired to go anymore, or by dying. And I thought I would stop someday and none of it would have mattered. I thought what would matter is saying something to future generations. I thought one day one of them would pick up a photograph and say, 'Here's our relation, Aunt Vicky,' and wonder what I was like. I used to wonder that all the time about pictures of my own family. Generations ago, my relatives were nonliterate. They couldn't have left a note for me."

My Dearest Grandchildren,

I would like to tell you as my grandmother told me . . .

Love God, family and your country, in that order. Always remember, you will know what type of parent you have been, not by your children, but by your grandchildren. You are, as I was, responsible for future generations. Do your best to make God, your family and your country as proud of your grandchildren as I am of mine.

> I love you,
> Your Grandmother
> *Gina Reece*
> TRYON, NORTH CAROLINA

⤳

Gina Reece comes from a family of Southern women. She grew up with a great-grandmother, a grandmother, a great-aunt, four aunts, a mother, four sisters and thirty-six cousins, thirty of whom are female.

"I was raised with a sense of family you do not find often in this modern world. If I remember nothing else my 'fore-mothers' said, the one thing that remains with me is 'Remember, you are raising your children for your grandchildren.'

"This note is the way it was told to me when I was expect-ing my first child, and as it was told to my mother, and told to my grandmother and to her mother and to her mother.

"Our family and our heritage are the last little hope we have for this world," she says. "Maybe thousands of years from now, people will be living off the land. We have twenty acres, so our five children will each have their acres of land, and maybe ten generations from now, when land is needed, each of our descendants will have a place to live, a place to build a house on. I'm big on the future."

Maybe you've been told you have your mother's eyes, your uncle's curiosity, your father's sense of humor. An inheritance is not necessarily a material asset, it is not always money, or jewelry, or land. An inheritance is the connection—your mother's eyes, your uncle's curiosity. It is what we've heard and what we've learned, what we've gained from our family and embraced as our own.

It is what ties us, both visibly and invisibly, to those who came before us.

It is recognizing ourselves as the embodiment of the dreams of generations gone.

It is a knowing, deep in the bones, that there is an uncrossable distance between right and wrong, which we measure from having the eyes of our mother.

From looking through her eyes.

From seeing the world as she would have us see it; a road, sometimes bumpy, yet paved with delight. A road meant to be traveled undauntedly while accompanied by worthy companions.

An inheritance is our unseeable soul.

It is our greatest fortune, earned without visible effort—from being loved, even before we were born.

Character is not an inheritance; each person must build it for himself or herself.

Betty Anderson
INDEPENDENCE, MISSOURI

୬୨

Betty Anderson is seventy-one. She has two children, four grandchildren and has lived, with her husband, in the same house for forty years.

"Considering all the generations, each one's lifetime is not that many years. Each life is a candle. My lifetime—no matter what it might be—is just a brief candle. We carry the torch for

a few years and then hand it over to our children, and our children's children.

"Each person has to develop his or her own character. But I do things so much like my own mother, and those are the things I want to pass along.

"And I want each generation to pass it on."

Dear Future Generations,

I have been asked to write a note to the future generations of my family and I have decided to accept the challenge—not without some degree of trepidation, however. For me to give advice would presume that I have great knowledge to impart. Unfortunately, such is not the case.

You and I are descended from a lot of hardworking, average people, who generally speaking were pretty nice to their fellow man. They believed in the Golden Rule and in doing their fair share.

You have inherited innate good common sense which should carry you through life's trials in good stead. It would be fascinating to know each and every one of you; but of course, each of us has only a short time on this Earth—truly a gift from God!

Should you come across a reference to me, either written or spoken, in the future, perhaps this letter will come to mind. Hopefully someday we'll all be together anyway. I shall truly greet you with open arms. You are truly loved even though you are now only a dream in my mind!

William E. Bennett
ELGIN, ILLINOIS

You will find a little something from me in your genes. Hope it doesn't leave you too short.

Joe Graves
MURRAY, KENTUCKY

Standards and Good Name

To All My Descendants:

The only personal possession that you actually own is your family name. Keep it unsullied, untarnished and as your statement to all who know you that you are a person of honesty and integrity. These attributes connected to your name will serve you well regardless of your station in life.

Gene Lowry
LAWRENCEVILLE, GEORGIA

∾

Gene Lowry is sixty-eight years old, born in the country and raised by farmers. He went to college and joined the Marine Corps. He went on to become a salesman with a national company.

He has moved back to his hometown—back to the sky of his childhood, he says.

"I'm looking at the same skies I looked at sixty-eight years ago.

"You can go out and buy anything else that anyone else has, but you keep your name in a lock box so it doesn't rust or corrode," he says. "I got that from my father and I think he got it from his father. I try to stress that to my boys and to the grandchildren. My children are raising their children like that. I think it took fairly well."

Gene Lowry's full name is Joseph Eugene Lowry. His father's name was Joseph and his grandfather's name was Joseph. His son's name is Joseph, as is the name of his grandson.

Hi Honey!

Just a note to let you know you're loved so much.

There are some things I want you to do and always remember.

First, remember who you are.

Set your standards high.

Keep the best company you can, and be selective of your friends. You are influenced by the company you keep.

Never allow anyone to change you or lower your standards.

Try to think good thoughts and keep a good sense of humor.

Live each day the very best you can.

Set your goals high, reach for those goals and they will be in your grasp.

Love always, Grandmother

Jean Jay
LIBERTY HILL, TEXAS

Jean Jay has lived in Texas all her life. She and her husband moved around because of his work in construction, but when the first of their three children was born they decided to settle in Liberty Hill. She is sixty-four.

"When my children started school, I did not want to move hither and yon. If you had a big diamond, you would not displace it. Children are our most precious jewels. They are our most valuable possessions.

"I told my children, first, remember who you are. It's so difficult in our culture for young people. They try to follow the crowd. I say, be who you are, not who someone else wants you to be."

To My Daughters . . .

Don't stoop to anyone's level! It's important to stand tall for your principles. Sometimes you'll look around and see you are the only one standing, but if in your heart you know you're right, I'll always stand alongside you.

Marilyn E. Woodard
RENO, NEVADA

The first words we learn to speak are "Mama" and "Papa." The first words we learn to write are our names. Our name is attached around our wrist in a bracelet when we are born. It is carved in stone and planted, claiming a piece of the earth when we die.

It is our flag upon the moon.

It is our calling.

Although it is chosen for us, we design and define it. We put it at the end of every piece of correspondence. When we sign our name, we give our word.

When those who know us hear our name, or see it, they immediately recognize all the nouns and verbs and adjectives of our lives, the millions of words that are compressed into our signature. Those nouns and verbs and adjectives swirl like script with a hundred meanings, but in the end, finally have just one.

Our names are us.

Two words or three, at least one of them shared with family, describing the ways we've spent the minutes and the hours and the days. All of our accomplishments, our attributes, attempts and good intent. Everything we've been taught and all we hope and stand for.

We could be lost in a crowd of thousands, and be found when we hear our name.

Dear Family,

As I have grown older, I more frequently think of the extended time spectrum during which mankind has inhabited this Earth. I view it as a large-stage, multiple-act production with each of us being bit players, struggling to learn our lines and hoping that when the spotlight falls on us for a brief time, our performance will be creditable and reflect dependable, tolerant, encouraging, honest, compassionate and loving persons who believe in God, who aggressively meet life's challenges and who work diligently to fulfill their dreams.

Much love always, Dad & Grandpa
Robert Baskin
KANSAS CITY, MISSOURI

Parent and Child

To my family:

My most fervent wish is that you will remember me as one who loved you unconditionally. One who looked for the good in you and focused on that. That each one of your faces is etched in my mind and heart like in a photograph album, and that as I go through that album, I remember the best in each one of you and say a special prayer that God will protect you from all danger and illness. That has always been my prayer for you, and that is also my prayer for those who are to come and join this family whether while I am still alive or not. Please feel my arms around you and the love I have for you.

Josie Pérez
CORPUS CHRISTI, TEXAS

෩

"We've raised some fine children. They turned out pretty good," says Josie Pérez. Her note on the kitchen table came easily, she says:

"It starts with my husband, Joe. We are Catholic and take our marriage vows very seriously. From the beginning of our marriage we had a special commitment to each other. As the years went by and we had our children, we also, as many others, had our shares of ups and downs. But Joe's commitment to our family never wavered. He has always worked hard at the post office, went to night school for ten years to get his degree of Bachelor of Arts, made time for family although it wasn't always easy. He always has been active in our parish, sings in the church choir and does things that are special to me like buying tickets to my favorite musical that's playing at the local playhouse. He brings my favorite sweet bread. Suggests that I call our daughter in Arizona even when he knows our long-distance bill is practically exhausted but knows how much I miss her and how happy calling her makes me. Takes me to see the bluebonnets, our state flower, in the spring, because he knows how their view fills me with wonderment. Takes me for a drive down the boulevard along the bay that he knows I love. I love him and hope that I am to him at least one tenth of all he is to me. This year we will be married thirty-four years.

"I know we are not the only family like this, as I am sure there exist many, many more. We do feel very blessed to have *such a fine family. In this day and age when the world is so different from when we were teenagers in the fifties, the bad outside influences have been there for our children. But I'd like to think that my husband and I, brothers and sisters, our church, our neighbors, aunts and uncles, cousins, friends and teachers have won out and have been an even larger influence on our children."*

To my children, and to theirs,

One day, a child of mine came home in tears. Another child had been mean to him and hurt his feelings. I want to say now, as I said then, "When a person doesn't like you, or is mean to you, it has more to do with them than it does with you. Dry your tears. You cannot be loved by everyone, because everyone cannot love themselves. You can know that I will always love you. And the greatest gift you can give to others is to love yourself. If you do that, you can love others without worrying whether they love you back. You will have enough love for both of you."

Dorothy L. Dupont
NORTH EASTON, MASSACHUSETTS

∽

Dorothy Dupont is fifty-four and has been an art director in the advertising business. Her mother grew up mother-less. This affected both Dorothy and her mother all of their lives.

"A parent is the first one to teach children love and to teach them that they're worthy of that love. This was a lesson my father taught me, and also taught my mother. He'd tell her, 'Dear, if they don't like you, it doesn't have anything to do with you.' He'd say, 'It has nothing to do with who you really are, it's how they perceive you to be.'"

If only our parents' faces were mirrors. If only we could see ourselves as they see us. Instead of all our hand-wringing and frustration, instead of banging our heads against the wall, we could look in that parental mirror and see what they see: learners in life, innocent travelers carrying suitcases they passed down to us, that their parents passed down to them, packed neatly and thoroughly, with clean clothes, an apple and an emergency flare.

Our parents know no one's perfect, and although they try to see perfection in us, they do not expect it of us. They want to light the way for us—

they would do it, if they could, from the light that shines in their eyes.

It is a soft light, like the one they kept turned on at night in the hallway, so we would feel no fear. The light on the porch, so we would find our way home. The light that reflects off our faces and back to them, eternal and lustrous. The light that they saw in their parents' eyes, and their parents saw in each other, and in their parents before them.

And before them. And before, and after, forever.

I tried to be a good mother by showing you the right path to follow, so please be careful when stepping on the narrow bridge of life.

Ruth Lachmann
ORANGE, CALIFORNIA

෮ඁ

Ruth Lachmann has three children and one grandchild. She is a Holocaust survivor.

"This note was from my personal experience. It's a warning.

"Society today doesn't have a road. Society needs some guidance. Life—you have it, now you don't. It's very fragile.

"In life, an accident can happen. Even the strongest building can be demolished. It's very difficult to choose a road. Especially for teenagers. Most people need guidance. I didn't have anybody to ask advice. I was all alone in the United States.

"You try to plan your life, and it could have so many unpredicted events. Life never ends the way you plan it. You have to make your decisions. Right road or wrong road."

My darling ones,

As I pen this note, I find myself filled with feelings of inadequacy. Have I taught you well? Have I taught you enough? Have I showed you through my actions, more than my teachings, that love is the most precious gift of all?

And I do love you all, much more than words or this silly letter could imply. Though the smell of perfume and my physical characteristics may fade from your memory, don't let go of God. I cannot take you through life any longer, but He will never leave you.

Connie Kris Hansen
Two Rivers, Wisconsin

I would like to say this to my children, grandchildren and their children:

Always be honest, trustworthy, caring, helpful, respectful and remember you can do anything you set your mind to do. Love the Lord with all your heart and soul, try and do a good deed each and every day you possibly can, get involved in your church, community and always be involved with all the things your children are doing. Take time to listen to them and eat at least one meal each day as a family.

For my life I hope that I have done exactly what the Lord wanted me to do. I have touched a lot of children by working with scouts, schools and, of course, church. I always saw what I could do for the sick, sent cards, visited, etc. I have had a very full life and hope all my children, grandchildren, on down the line, can say the same thing.

Mrs. C. W. Thomalla
Ashland City, Tennessee

∽

Mrs. Thomalla is sixty-eight and her husband is seventy-eight. He was in the Army when their five children were growing up.

"We knew we could not have breakfast together. We knew we could not have lunch together. But at dinner, all the children would sit down with Daddy and Mother and we'd talk about what was going on."

They would talk about what was taking place in the community, in the country, in their lives, in the world.

"Dinner was the time to get your opinion in," she says.

Still now, on Sundays, some of the children will come to eat, and the grandchildren will join in the discussion about what's going on.

Dear Sara, Shaelyn, Micah . . .
Sean and Julie . . .
And your future children . . .
And their children . . . and theirs:

When I was a young mother, with three small children, I remember reading a simple short sentence that I ran across in some book or magazine. I don't remember the source, or anything else about the article in which it appeared. But it had such an impact on me, and it made such an impression, that I always remembered it, and have tried to live by it. This is the sentence I read:

People are more important than things.

It sounds so simple, but when you think about it, that really says a lot. To me, one of the things it meant was: if I had a dirty house waiting to be cleaned, but the morning dawned bright and sunny, and I thought we needed an outing more than the house needed a cleaning, then I took my kids to the park instead. Children will remember playing in the warm sunshine, with their mom pushing them on the swings, much more than they will recall how dust-free the furniture looked that day.

There is also a broader meaning to that sentence that I read so long ago. It is this: to cherish and tend to the relationships with the people who mean the most to you is much more important than the acquisition of material possessions or than spending too much time climbing the ladder of your career.

Of course, there's a place for those things, but what holds the highest meaning in life is the sharing of yourself and the giving of your love. This can be manifested in the encouraging words spoken and the hugs given to a spouse, or a child, or a friend who is feeling a little "down." And it's shown in the word of appreciation and acknowledgment that means you've noticed when they have done something well or accomplished something special. Or even if they've just tried hard and need to be noticed.

It means taking the time to say "Thank you," or "I'm sorry," or "You sure look great today." It means being an encourager and not a criticizer.

It all comes down to what happens when you love and care about people.

All my love, Grandma Gay
Gay Sorensen
OLYMPIA, WASHINGTON

Gay Sorensen has a hard time critiquing people. Even in a writing class, she would rather make a suggestion than a criticism.

"I'll say, 'Here's a little way you might make things better, but this part I really loved,'" she says.

She is seventy and semi-retired. She used to work as an executive secretary, but is now a part-time nanny. The little boy and girl she looks after are five and seven.

"Last year I helped them write little books. They drew pictures and I wrote down what they told me about the pictures. That book was called The Magical House in the Forest.*"*

This year, she says the children wrote their own stories. "Bugs in Space" was one, "Erica the Rabbit," the other.

The children's mother is a preschool administrator. She was so mightily impressed with Gay Sorensen's endeavors she is taking the books around to a multitude of preschools as an example of an exercise to build children's self-esteem.

"I didn't even realize I was doing that," Mrs. Sorensen says. "I guess I've made a habit of complimenting people for their efforts, and when I do they make more of an effort."

And this is the way the world can be built. Treating a heart like a ruby. Treating an idea as if it were Baby Einstein's.

Habitually. Every day. One person at a time.

To all my children:

If, in all the things I have tried to bring to you as a parent, I have failed to make you realize you have value—or, to put it another way, if you lack self-esteem or self-worth—I have failed you.

> So know it now!
> *Doris Dombrowski*
> COUNTRY CLUB HILLS, ILLINOIS

Remember, Kids:

Even when I am mad at you, I what? Still love you!

> xo xo xo
> Love, Mom
> *Elizabeth M. Rusiniak*
> LANSING, ILLINOIS

∾

Elizabeth Rusiniak is forty-five, a nurse, and has lived her whole life in Illinois. She has three children.

"I've always said that to them, if they're fighting, whatever it may be, so we never go to bed mad. I say, 'I what?,' and, mad as they are, they say it.

" 'Still love you!'

"I've been doing this since they've been born. It's something they know is so important, they'll probably say it to their own kids."

M o t h e r   S a i d

To My Children, Grandchildren and Great-Grandchildren,

At seventy-three, I am enjoying the peace of mind that is the fruit of trusting in my mother's wisdom and following her advice.

She said, "Keep out of other people's disputes, whether they be friends or family. They will eventually patch up their disagreements, and any comments you have made will come home to haunt you."

Mollie F. Howard
El Paso, Texas

Unfortunately, my paternal grandmother passed away last week. We found a note in her address book:

A smile is a whisper of a laugh.

Andrea L. Buege
Menomonee Falls, Wisconsin

Our parents' voices are the songs that are stuck in our heads. The ones we've been singing all day, without even knowing it.

Sometimes we even hear that which cannot be

33

heard: the way they'd shake their heads before starting to speak. Suddenly we are back to the time and place and circumstance that would evoke this familiar action.

We not only watch our parents, we absorb them. Their words, their deeds and gestures become part of us, sure as bones.

At times this strikes us as close to comical. More often it is as comforting as a heartbeat.

When we hear these voices, we hear a clear-sung chorus. A love song on the radio you've heard so many times, in so many pleasant places, that it's your all-time favorite.

An ever present echo, the gentle, persistent lullaby of raindrop on rock.

There isn't a day goes by that I don't think of my mother and her sayings. She had values that she tried to instill in us; she taught us how to treat others, and good manners, table and otherwise.

Today I sometimes wonder if I stressed these values enough in my own children. Much of what I always felt was important seems to have gotten lost in today's society.

I wish I had put a note on my kitchen table for my children to read, and to pass on to the grandchildren. It would contain the teachings that I will always dearly thank my own mother for.

Besides the Golden Rule of treating others as you wished to be treated yourself, she had such advice as "Don't tarry (hang around) where you aren't welcomed" and "Keep your hands off things that don't belong to you." My children heard these enough times, but I don't believe I ever put it in writing.

My mother had many delightful sayings and I never did know where she got them. Two of my favorites were "Much wants more" (someone who has a lot but is never satisfied) and "Either one would spoil another couple" (said about two "dysfunctional" people who belonged to-gether—though you wonder how they ever managed to find one another!).

Margaret Lev
ARLINGTON HEIGHTS, ILLINOIS

❧

Margaret Lev is seventy-two. She was raised in Chicago, but traveled during the war. Her husband passed away in 1973. She has five children and two grandchildren.

"It's funny what comes to you out of the blue," she says. "We don't realize what impact our parents had on our lives."

She has repeated her mother's numerous sayings so many times in her own house, her son once asked her why she didn't put them in a book.

"Your mother said everything!" he told her.

Don't worry about tomorrow, because tomorrow will worry about itself. Each day has enough worries of its own.

Donna C. Schneider
MILWAUKEE, WISCONSIN

ᖰᖱ

Donna Schneider is sixty-seven and about to move from the house she's lived in for forty-two years. She has five children and eleven grandchildren.

"This is something my dad instilled in me," she says. "He used to be sick a lot and worried about when the end of his life would come. And he'd tell me this was not the right way to be. You do things today and try to do them the best you can. The past is gone. Try not to worry."

The enclosed is actually the note my mother wrote in the back of the book *To Our Children's Children* she filled out for me. The note reflects the exact ideology of my mother; dedicated, complex, simple, strong, caring, loving and ever giving. Her mother, my grandmother, passed on the other note I have included. She lived her life within its contents. I cherish the words daily.

Amy Squires
SAN FRANCISCO, CALIFORNIA

From my mother, Susan Squires, Chicago, Illinois:

When you're young, you can't wait until you are old enough to start school, drive a car, have your own apartment, etc. In time, however, you realize time flies and life speeds along. Anticipation is half the joy, but you don't understand that until later in life.

To me, balance is the key. Make time for family, relationships, friends, love, work that is meaningful, make time to reflect and read and be alone, and time to play. Give something back to society.

If you can achieve this balance you will have achieved what most of us cannot—but what a noble try it will be.

I will love you always,
Mom

From my grandmother, Lois Holley Busick, Normal, Illinois (deceased):

"How far you go in life depends on your being tender with the young; compassionate with the aged; sympathetic of the striving and tolerant of the weak and the strong. Because someday in life you will have been all of these."

—George Washington Carver

Amy Squires is thirty and lives in San Francisco. She is an online editor. Her mother worked as a nurse practitioner.

"My grandmother passed away the day after I graduated from high school," she says. "She was always a great letter writer. She moved to California when my sister and I were very young. She'd write us letters every week. Mom has them all.

"She sent me this quote when I was little. It was her favorite."

Irreplaceable Now

Enjoy today. It can never be replaced.

Rosanne Armstrong
PITTSBURGH, PENNSYLVANIA

∽

Rosanne Armstrong is thirty-five and has six children: three teenagers from her first marriage, three babies from her current marriage.

"This is the meat of everything," she says. "Things are so complicated these days. We pack seventeen, eighteen hours into every day. Life moves so fast. My mother can remember having time for her kids, time for the neighbors. I have three kids under the age of three. The days are a blur. But even on bad days, I say, enjoy this stage. It's one stage in a cycle, and there are thousands of cycles. No days are the same. You can't recapture this moment."

A legacy to my beloved family:

A wish for you to live each day to its fullest and do all you can to make each day the best day ever. Keep God in your heart and let Him be your guide in all your plans for living a life fulfilled with happiness. God bless each and every one from Your Grandmother Mary

Mary Harris
MUSCATINE, IOWA

To the future generations of our family:
Something to consider
(which you might find useful):

Throughout the history of the world, there have been many people who claimed to possess the secret to a happy and successful life, and have insisted that if others followed their recipe, the same result will follow. While there is no doubt that these "secrets" have their merit, it has been my experience that no one person is qualified to tell anyone else how to live his or her life. Life is purely subjective and relative to the circumstances we find ourselves in. What works for one may not necessarily work for another.

And with that auspicious prologue, let me now pass on to you, my descendants, what I have learned about life and the pursuit of happiness and success. While I don't claim to guarantee that these "secrets" will work for you, I do think they are worth sharing. You might find that you can adjust them to suit your particular life course.

The first, and most important, thing I learned about life is that everything we do affects everything around us. If we remember that every action and choice we make has a consequence, whether good or bad, we avoid going through life in a directionless daze.

In the world of physics, there is a theory that describes this: the Butterfly Effect. The theory says that a butterfly flapping its wings in Singapore can cause a hurricane somewhere in Kansas. While this seems incredible on the surface, it really does make a lot of sense. Everything in the universe is interconnected, including every living thing. A simple thing like a butterfly flapping its wings can cause just enough of a ripple in the air around it that it causes a chain reaction of ripples that eventually cause a storm.

It is the same with our actions. Even the smallest action, like smiling at a stranger on a street, can cause a chain reaction of feelings that mushrooms and eventually spreads across the entire world.

It is why wars are started. War never begins over a major episode; it is a series of small, sometimes minuscule, actions that explode into brother killing brother. Amazing to think that the opposite could equally be true.

True world peace could be achieved through a series of small kindnesses to each other. If you do nothing else in your lives, remember that everything you do counts, so act accordingly.

Related to that thought is the second philosophy I live by, which is that humans worry too much. We worry so much, in fact, that we waste precious minutes, hours, days and years of a life that could offer us so much, if we only took the time to live it! Most, if not all, of what we worry about in our lives is simply not worth the effort. Once we stop worrying and making ourselves crazy, we find that life wins out anyway. Things always have a way of falling into place and turning out right. Remember the first "secret" and combine it with the second, and you'll realize just how easy it is to stop worrying about things that don't matter.

The world and life do not stop hurtling toward the future because we have a problem. What does stop, however, is our ability to delight in that forward motion.

And the last little "secret" I have learned through living is that we must all take time to just be.

Awareness, taking time to really enjoy and savor the moment we're living in, is so important. Too, too many of us are so busy thinking about the future or the past that we don't ever experience the present. If you are taking a walk, take a walk—smell the air, listen to the birds, marvel at the blueness of the sky, feel the ground under your feet. Don't think about the dinner you have to cook later, the bills you have to pay, the laundry you have to pick up, the homework you have to do, the telephone call you have to return. For when we do think about those things, we have lost the moment forever.

And the only way we can try to recapture it is by thinking about the past. It then becomes a vicious cycle, and we find at the end of our lives that we never really lived, because we weren't ever there.

> We were always someplace else.
> We are beings, so we must learn to be.
> *Diana Dominguez*
> BROWNSVILLE, TEXAS

୧୭

Diana Dominguez is thirty-seven, a high school and college teacher.

"I try to teach this to my kids in school. I try to make a point, even when I'm upset, that they never leave the classroom thinking that I'm upset with them. The seniors in high school are at a point in their lives where they have to make major decisions. I'm the last person to give them nurturing before the big, bad world. All seventeen-year-olds think they're immortal. That they can do anything. I try to impart to them that the thing they have to learn is that everything you do leaves traces behind. Everything they do. Everybody they touch.

"I have to send eighty kids every year off into the wide world."

So many of our memories are formed by snapshots of special occasions. Sometimes, with no written record of a family history, snapshots are what we have to base our memories on.

And snapshots, through the ages, have been rather formal affairs. While we now capture our families on film wearing flip-flops and cutoffs, our ancestors, in our mind's memory, are attending rural picnics in top hats and summer gowns.

In those faraway frozen moments, wearing those top hats and bonnets, these were real folks, sitting on blankets once, enjoying peaches warmed by the sun.

That was their now. That was their moment. They were not thinking of being pasted in a scrapbook. They were passing the finger sandwiches and sweet lemonade.

All this means is, there doesn't have to be a snapshot. There doesn't have to be an outing. What there has to be is the moment. Even when the moment is doing the dishes—or reading the Sunday morning paper in bed.

Every day is not a picnic. But every day is what we're doing. Savor the irreplaceable now.

After losing a much wanted baby at ten weeks into the pregnancy, and then living one and a half years with an undiagnosed ailment of my husband's, I really thought about what note I would leave. Living day to day, not knowing what my husband's condition would be or how much it would worsen, I found that life and love became precious! I learned what really was important and what wasn't.

He is now treated and cured. I am so thankful the trial is over, but I am also thankful I have the knowledge from it. This is the background that urged me to share my note on the kitchen table.

Dear Loved One:

Live each day as if it were your last.
Don't do everything, just the important things.
Laugh with those who rejoice,
Cry with those who hurt,
Be thankful for the blessings you have,
And give all your problems to God, for He does answer prayers.

Lisa Cuthbert
HAMILTON, ONTARIO, CANADA

The gift of life is something to be treasured. It should be enjoyed in a moral and responsible manner.

Harold Barlow
RAYTOWN, MISSOURI

Creativity and Imagination

Remember
To listen to the flowers . . .
To taste the rainbows . . .
To embrace the song that makes you uniquely you.

Thomas P. O'Hay

MEMPHIS, TENNESSEE

༖

Thomas P. O'Hay is sixty-one and has been married for forty years. He has five children and nine grandchildren.

" 'Listen to the flowers?' my children used to ask me when I gave them this advice. They'd say, 'I can smell the flowers. I can touch the flowers.' The lesson is listen to the flowers. The flowers will tell you what makes them grow. They need rain as well as sunshine. They don't need just sunshine all the time.

"You have to take the bad with the good. If there weren't any bad times you would not appreciate the good.

"Taste the rainbows? So many times you just see something, observe something, you don't really become immersed in the world.

"One time we were looking at a rainbow. One of the kids said it reminded them of sherbet. We went inside and ate rainbow sherbet.

"You've got to enjoy the little things in this life. I tried to get my kids to stretch their minds. I thought the best thing I could give them would be a great vivid imagination."

Creativity is nothing more than the act of looking at things in a different way.

Imagination is the tool, the fuel.

Imagination comes naturally—it was installed at the factory. We first noticed it in ourselves as children when we sat astonished at how red paint bubbled when brushed next to yellow.

We had direct access then.

It's still there.

Without it, life can be a movie without a sound track. Small moments happen along, but at weary times it can be difficult to care. Add a little imagination and the movie starts to soar, to pirouette and curtsy.

Life is train travel—not all passage and carriage. It is single scenes, one at a time, out the window. Laundry hanging on a line. A warehouse. The river's shores.

Each sight out the window has hundreds of stories behind it. And hundreds of stories before those hundreds of stories began.

The rose, made of sugar, on the icing, on the cake.

Get as much education as possible, go to the church of your choice and follow the Ten Commandments. Do everything in moderation, travel and take time to sit and dream.

Dorothy E. O'Malley
MERRILLVILLE, INDIANA

Quotes

Here is a passage from William Blake I have always kept in my personal cookbook, and I would like to see it left on my kitchen table when I am gone:

"To see a world in a grain of sand
And a heaven in a wild flower,
Hold infinity in the palm of your hand
And eternity in an hour."

Liz Burke
MERCER ISLAND, WASHINGTON

∾

Liz Burke is forty-three, an "executive mother in transition" of a first grader and a two-year-old. Previously she was a lawyer, an environmental consultant and a roofer.

"I keep that quote in the beginning of my cookbook, a cookbook of recipes I have collected from friends. It's in the first page, in that little plastic place where you would have a recipe.

"I collect quotes along with recipes. Actually recipes are more of a sideline."

51

She has had the quote for years, probably since college. That's when she first copied it in her own hand. She has held on to it ever since, stashing it where she will see it.

"It makes me enjoy cooking much more. When you're cooking, you're doing something important, although it does not seem important at the time."

Liz Burke has learned to fly, as well as cook some, while between careers.

"You're thinking about your problems, and at thirty thousand feet the world is a grain of sand. Even a person looks like a grain of sand. Find the beauty."

We've all had the experience of reading something, or hearing something, that speaks to us so completely the words may as well have called out our name.

These are true moments of connection, when we feel understood and agreed with; we feel inspired and moved and made strong. This is the beauty and the power of words; the fact that a phrase, or a sentence, a poem or lyric, can speak for more than one heart.

When we find these treasures made of words, we consider them personal sermons.

They are secrets whispered to us from a friend

we've never met. We go for the scissors or fountain pen, to cut them out or copy them and claim them for our own.

We tuck them away in places where we're sure to come back upon them or post them proudly where they will meet our eyes every day. They become our thresholds. We commit them to memory; we repeat them to our family and friends as inspiration, reminder or gift.

We carry them in our wallets. They are as identifying as a driver's license.

We scoop them from the air. They are butterflies we can hold on to forever, words caught as shimmering beauty in our net.

"Thank God every morning when you get up that you have something to do that day, which must be done, whether you like it or not. Being forced to work, and forced to do your best will breed in you temperance and self control, diligence and strength of will, cheerfulness and content, and a hundred virtues which the idle never know."

—Charles Kingsley
Marion Jean Larson
OAK BROOK, ILLINOIS

I have a favorite saying (thought, philosophy, whatever). It isn't original, but I love it.

"You don't drown from falling in the water, you drown from staying there."

It's a good lesson that I hope all my offspring will learn!

Joan Chrzanowski
SPRINGFIELD, MASSACHUSETTS

I'm only twenty-three, but . . . these are phrases, funny and motivational, I had taped on the walls of my bedroom at my parents' home. Now, I've moved out on my own, and am getting married. These words to live by still stay with me and hopefully will as I enter this new phase of my life. My fiancé asked, "In our apartment, will you still put inspirational sayings around?" I hope so! I like them! And we'll be passing on our words of wisdom to our children in the coming years.

Remember, nobody appreciates self-righteousness.
"There's nobody better than you in this world
And you're no better than anyone else."

Remember, be open to others.
"Sometimes you just gotta take the cotton out of your ears and put it in your mouth."

Remember, life isn't always smooth.
"If you can laugh at it, you can live with it."

Remember, have fun.
"Act a little crazy,
Make things worthwhile.
Then remember your friends
With a laugh and a smile."

Remember, we all must strive.
"We ain't what we should be,
We ain't what we're gonna be,
But, at least, we ain't what we was."

I don't take credit for coining any of these, but the beauty is in the fact they were out there for me to hear. May we all open our hearts.

Jennifer K. Barrett
CLARENDON HILLS, ILLINOIS

L i s t s

To our children and their children:

I leave you with Ten Commandments besides those given to Moses by God.

1. Spread a little good cheer to those around you.
2. Try harder to tolerate those you may not like.
3. Develop honesty and integrity.
4. Trust God to know what is good for you, even though you may not agree with Him.
5. If you think you may have failed in something, analyze it and learn from it.
6. Financial security is important. Earn your money honestly, invest it wisely, spend it frugally and share some of it with others in a prudent manner.
7. Never lose sight of why you have been put on this Earth.
8. If you have a special talent, try to share it with others, but above all, exploit it yourself as far as you can.
9. When you are faced with adversity: Blow your nose;

pull up your socks; square your shoulders and face it like your grandmother would have faced it.

10. Smile!

Don Terrien

NAPERVILLE, ILLINOIS

◌◦

Don Terrien, at seventy, has lived in Naperville for thirty years and has been married to Allegra, whom everyone calls Dorrie, for forty-eight years. He worked for the same company for forty years. The Terriens have three children and five grandchildren. After his retirement, Mr. Terrien did volunteer work, with detectives, at the arboretum, even helping little children across the street.

"Put God first," he says. "That's the reason you're here. Live honestly and forthrightly. It is necessary to fashion a life of integrity. That's about the size of it."

And as far as facing things as your grandmother would have?

That's an ode to Mrs. Terrien's grandmother, Belle.

"Her attitude was 'Upward and forward,'" Dorrie Terrien says. "It was tough to grow up that long ago. It took tremendous strength. She took me in, and raised me,

58

which was a blessing. She was an amazingly open-minded person."

Could she ever have known, that all these years later, her granddaughter's husband would consider her attributes ones he would like to pass along?

Our beliefs and attributes can blend, over the years, with those of others to whom we're connected.

As Don Terrien would say: That's about the size of it.

And in a family, down through the ages, that size is likely to grow.

To my descendants: Six maxims to guide your life:

1. Cherish your extended family and act accordingly.
2. Read, read, read to nourish your mind, heart and soul.
3. You will not find peace, love, happiness or fulfillment by looking in the mirror, but only by looking out various windows to the world and acting positively on the needs you see.
4. If you must choose between getting a job done or getting credit for it, get the job done.
5. Avoid court encounters if at all possible, as they always ruin the tranquility of life and often your wealth.
6. Be a weight to none and a buoy to all.

Ronald L. Rindge
MOORPARK, CALIFORNIA

59

Ronald Rindge was born in Los Angeles in 1934. He and his wife Sue were married in 1956 and have six children and thirteen grandchildren. His career was accounting.

"The six maxims I settled on were easy to compile. I asked myself, What principles of daily living have given Sue and me a happy, fulfilling life? A close, mutually supportive and respectful family environment, a family whose members respect and support each other in good times and bad is the bedrock of our lives. So, if it worked well for us, it seems it should work also for our children's children, if practiced!

"The maxim about avoiding lawsuits if at all possible is rooted in the obvious: contentious events destroy the tranquility of life and can ruin your health and wealth.

"Sometimes lawsuits are necessary. Each person has to ask himself, Do I really need to win this argument or money legally, no matter the cost, or is it better to avoid the tensions and uncertainties pursuing a goal through the courts that is not crucial to my life? The natural desire to protect one's rights should be weighed against the many burdens one picks up along the legal road to judgment, which often may be a dead end or a hidden chasm.

"The maxim 'Be a weight to none but a buoy to all' is one from my grandfather, Frederick Hastings Rindge. I do not know if he originated it or discovered this principle of life from another. It is somewhat similar to the adage 'If you can't say something nice, don't say anything at all.' In other words, if you cannot lift up other's lives, at least do not do anything to weigh them down. Your spirits will be buoyant if you make a practice of encouraging and cheering on others."

Here are my suggestions that I would leave to my family:
1. Honesty
2. Integrity
3. Education
4. Pray daily
5. Kindness to self and others
6. Learn to laugh at self before others do
7. Learn empathy
8. Really listen to others, even the dull and the ignorant
9. Learn body language
10. Learn work ethic
11. Try to practice the Golden Rule daily
12. Don't be a spendthrift, neither be miserly
13. Humor can help or heal situations
14. Worship together if possible
15. Repay debts of gratitude

16. Honor parents, grandparents and ancestors
17. Accept people as they are
18. If there is a spouse or lover, really try to love, listen, share, comfort and appreciate that person in good times and bad until these things can no longer be done
19. Never blame or make children suffer for whatever one parent may have done wrong
20. Show and teach children strength, fairness, tolerance and equality
21. Teach children how to aspire and achieve, alone or together with others
22. Pride for self and country
23. Respect other people's rights, differences, customs and cultures
24. Do not label or stigmatize people
25. Do not stereotype people
26. Have self-confidence
27. Do not accuse others wrongfully
28. Have compassion for self and others
29. Love and be truthful to thyself first, only then can you love and be truthful to others, and then people will love and be truthful to you in return
30. Above all, be a good citizen

Mrs. Irma LeCadre Chase
New York, New York

᠙

*Irma LeCadre Chase is sixty-two and has one daughter
who has received her doctorate in law. Mrs. Chase was born in
Trinidad in the West Indies, but has lived in the United States
for forty-five years. She worked as a registered nurse. She is now
legally blind. She wrote her list on the envelopes of unopened
magazines.*

*She put body language on her list because she thinks body
language can save you so much time.*

"In nursing, sometimes someone's body might be telling
you one thing while their mouth is telling you another," she
says. "They might be tense, and they're telling you, 'No, no, I'm
relaxed,' but their arms might be crossed, and their legs crossed
tight.

"When we came to this country, honestly, I couldn't understand segregation. Here we are, in the biggest country, the
richest country, so forward in so many things, so backward in
the way people treated their own people! In the West Indies, it's
such a mixture. In my family there are African, Scottish,
French, Indian, Japanese. You name it, we got it. When people
say colors of the rainbow, we live the colors of the rainbow in

my family. We believe in Buddhism. We practice what we preach.

"A lot of things on this list, I heard from my mother. I heard them from the age of three, and these are the things my daughter has heard from me. You are told these things, but sometimes you have to write them down to see them. You have to see them in print. You tend to remember them longer."

Irma LeCadre Chase, having lost much of her ability to see, is teaching herself to read again using computer programs for the blind.

From Moses to Stephen R. Covey, everybody likes a list. Why? Because lists make the difficult seem doable. One thing at a time, step by step.

First this, then this, then that, then the other.

Just checking an item off becomes an attainable goal—you aim for that check, that crossing off, that private satisfaction.

Lists break down the huge, tame the nebulous. They offer format and order.

How many times have you found a list in your pocket, of the things you needed from the hardware store last week, or the ingredients for last night's dinner? And you look at it and see something already taken care of. Something accomplished, maybe memorable, maybe not. But something that weighed on your mind for a moment, then gave way to a tiny pat on the back and a small congratulation.

Another step on another day, maybe just another errand on the errand-go-round. But something that, item by item, thing by thing, moved the daily miracle/endurance contest of family life along.

Dear Friend,

Be happy.
Don't hurt other people.
Hope that you fall in love.
With best wishes,

Deb Carmody
HIGHTSTOWN, NEW JERSEY

৯৹

Deb Carmody wasn't married at the time she sent her Note on the Kitchen Table, although she knew her future husband was a special kind of man. She is twenty-five years old and pursuing her MBA. She works as a computer programmer.

Her note was actually something she heard on a television situation comedy. When she was in high school, the message pleased her so, she wrote the words on a piece of paper. She put it in her journal. When she went off to college, she took the quote with her and tacked it on her bulletin board.

"It was just this little piece of paper, and on it was all I wanted out of life."

Her marriage is going wonderfully, by the way.

Three out of three for Deb Carmody.

Three wishes she's had since high school.

Three wishes she's attained.

Whoever reads this note:

Be honest and happy. Do not be a phony or put on airs. Try to be helpful as much as you can. Be optimistic. A sense of humor is always healthy. Enjoy life as it comes. Accept criticism and learn by your mistakes. Try your best to think of something new at least once a week. Your partner deserves a change!

Theresa M. Ridgley
GAITHERSBURG, MARYLAND

Do Unto Others

Always treat others the way you want to be treated. If you're doing something that is not some way you would want to be treated, then you shouldn't be doing it.

M. Kathryn McAdams
GEORGETOWN, TEXAS

Be ye kind to one another, always.

Jeanette A. Kimball
VAN NUYS, CALIFORNIA

Before you make any decisions or take any actions, examine your motives. Let the Golden Rule be your guide in all you do.

Rebecca J. Janes
TERREBONNE, OREGON

We need to be kind to everyone we meet. We are all fighting difficult battles. Some cover it better than others, but we need to take a moment to look deep in the other person's heart. More than likely there is pain and our kindness can help ease their burden.

Linda K. Arnold
OREM, UTAH

Linda Arnold is thirty-eight and was raised in Califor-nia. She has two daughters and has been married for fifteen years.

"I wrote this because I feel I've been harshly judged on occasion. If people knew what was going on inside another person, inside that person's heart, maybe they'd be less judgmental.

"We live in a nice neighborhood. I look across the street and see people who seem to have it so together. Then come to find out, one family lost two children, another lost one. Nobody gets off unscathed. If we're more patient and more kind with one another, this world will be an easier place to live."

The popularity of ball games, and board games, and even computer games stems from a prescribed set of circumstances. These circumstances are called the rules. They are arbitrary, and devised from someone's imagination. Yet they are adhered to, most rigidly, or the game would not, could not exist.

Why, then, is the Golden Rule—so simple, so elemental—not followed quite so doggedly? What could be easier than behaving toward others as we would have them behave toward us?

> There is nothing to study in this. It takes no real skill, no extraordinary coordination, no quickness of mind or hand.
>
> Nothing has to be memorized. There is no need for practice.
>
> Would this feel good for me? If not, then it would not feel good for you.
>
> Exceedingly easy. Blinding with glory. And without it, the game is called because of darkness.

You should take this life very seriously, but don't let it be a drudgery. Take this life with a smile, but don't let it be frivolous. Be kind to people. It will come back to you. Be generous. That, too, will come back to you. Selfishness will make you miserable. Above all, be compassionate.

Jesse Paine
Whitney, Texas

❦

Jesse Paine is seventy-two and semiretired after a lifetime of selling business machines. He is married for the second time.

"Primarily, the experiences I had through life I took too seriously. I had five kids to raise and was intensely trying, not only to get ahead but to make ends meet. I didn't come up in an easy manner. And at this age, I'm more conscious of com-

passion and the difference it makes in a house. I've begun to show compassion, only because I've lately been exposed to it."

Be sweet to each other.

Robert and Curtsy Thompson
VANCOUVER, WASHINGTON

Be true to yourself and always remember, what goes around, comes around.

Sue R. Blundell
MANDEVILLE, LOUISIANA

༄

Sue Blundell is sixty-five and has four children and six grandchildren: five grandsons and one brand-new baby granddaughter.

"I just think, by the grace of God, you are who you are," she says. *"I've had an awful lot of luck in my life, and I think some of that luck comes from my trying to be good.*

"I feel that if you do something nice, it will eventually come back to you, and if you don't do something nice, that will come back to you, too. What you give is going to come back to you.

"But don't be afraid you're going to lose those things you

feel so lucky about. We had an apartment building that blew down in a hurricane. It was not important. It was only a building.

"Your family, your health . . . This is a lovely life. Count your blessings. We all have so many."

Know that when you look into another person's face, into their eyes, child or adult, that you always see your own reflection.

That person is you. See him from deep inside your soul, not from your mind. Listen to him or her, hear them, validate them. We are all one, no more, no less.

Try not to judge although sometimes it may be difficult.

More than happiness, seek peace.

Tillie Summers
MORTON GROVE, ILLINOIS

To my children:

I must leave you soon
And this you know
There comes a time
We all must go
When you miss me look to one another
For part of me is in your sister and brother

Lend your neighbors a helping hand
Always be kind to your fellow man
For this is what life is meant to be
And what would mean the most to me

> All my love always,
> Mother
> *Mary Joan Richards*
> BEULAH, MICHIGAN

Follow the Golden Rule: Do unto others as you would have them do unto you.

> *June Jackson*
> GAINESVILLE, FLORIDA

F r i e n d s

I would like to leave the secret of a good life to my grandchildren. Laugh at yourself. Have a sense of humor. Have empathy for others. Try to volunteer whenever you can. Give someone an honest compliment every day. I do all these things and I have tons of friends. Whenever anyone hurts me, I come back with love. Turn the other cheek.

Elaine Kerin
PITTSBURGH, PENNSYLVANIA

෧෨

Elaine Kerin has lived in Pittsburgh all her life. She is eighty-one. She has two sons and six grandchildren.

"I tell jokes to everybody," she says. "I do try to give a compliment every day. If I'm bowling or anything, and I see someone with a nice blouse, I mention it. If her hair looks nice, I mention it. I think we're put on Earth not only to enjoy ourselves, but to make other people happy. I just try to do what I can to make life pleasant. Spread the love around.

"You have to throw your bread on the water to get French toast back."

Don't judge people. Show patience and understanding toward people in your life, whether you feel they deserve it or not. Don't pretend to understand how others feel when only they know for sure. Just be a friend and give support.

Marian E. Moore
BOWLING GREEN, OHIO

To My Family,

Always be proud of who and what you are. If and when you become parents, teach your children to have good character and family pride. When you establish your own home, be good neighbors, friendly, cheerful and helpful if needed. My fondest hope for all of you is that you will always be happy and know without a doubt that you are loved so very, very much by Grandma.

Marie Clark
BEAVERTON, OREGON

Friends are the family members you would never find in a genealogical search, nor fill a space for on an ancestral chart. Friends are not branches on the family tree; they are the leaves that embellish the space between the branches with fresh, invigorating green.

Our friends are not in our bloodline, but they make up our lifeline—extending a hand, an ear, a shoulder, sharing a big horse laugh.

Country of origin for a friend? Work. Class at the Y. The PTA. Maybe the house next door, or the one across the street.

You can meet a friend in first grade and keep her all your life. You can meet a friend at the Senior Center and share that first-grade friend with him, as you paint a picture of what went on before.

A friend is one to whom you send clippings, one who calls you long-distance. A friend suggests books to read and alerts you when asparagus is on sale.

You can complain about your family to a friend. A friend attends your family's funerals.

Friends tell you the truth, in ways they think you can stand to hear.

A friend is someone who does not have to love you, but loves you.

Lead an honest life and take care of each other. Keep up your faith. God will reward you for your kindness. Forgive those who hurt or betray you and be the first to make friends again.

Mrs. Marie Kadavy
DWIGHT, NEBRASKA

Next to your parents, as you grow older, your friends can be a great source of comfort, fun and camaraderie. In some ways, friends can be more important than family. A lack of close friends truly leaves a void that cannot be filled. A true friend would do just about anything for you—a rare commodity. Choose your friends wisely; you are truly known by the friends that you keep.

William E. Bennett
ELGIN, ILLINOIS

Respect and Tolerance

Do not hypocrocise your values and beliefs. Be honest and respectful of others, but first and foremost be honest and respectful to yourself.

Linda Newcomb
URBANA, ILLINOIS

The one word that has affected my life the most—love. Loving yourself and loving your neighbor would solve so many problems, whether it be family or world problems. Just loving people and accepting them, not trying to change them. Living in the now moment—being so completely absorbed in that one moment and having the time of your life, just as a child lives one moment at a time. To live each day as if it were your last. To live this way is what God had in mind.

I truly believe if each of us did just these few things the world would be a different place.

Harriet Cole
ALLEN PARK, MICHIGAN

My dear girls,

I am purposely placing this note in the kitchen, where I know, after all the checking in other areas, this will be the last place you will look. I base this theory on your aversion to kitchens and kitchen work as children.

By placing this most important message here in the kitchen, I assure that it will remain in your thoughts and not become scrambled with all the earlier details of dissemination.

God created and gave us a beautiful world. Unfortunately as we grew and became wiser in advanced technology we became "dumber" about conserving and preservation. Until now, the concern becomes whether man will literally destroy not only himself, but the world as well.

Hence, my dear children, the war cry is Recycle! Take old worn-out things and ideas, and make them new. It's more difficult to mend than to create. While we should be concerned about the physical world in which we live, the broken emotions, dreams, spirit and morals of today's society should also be repaired.

I'm asking each of you to "recycle" minds that are intolerant of other races and creeds into useful contributing entities of awareness.

Recycle actions of ugliness toward others into positive and genuine friendship and understanding.

Recycle those who would ignore and demean our handicapped into persons with compassion and understanding that "There, but for the grace of God, go I."

Recycle, my dears, Recycle! Help restore our world back into the Eden it once was.

Mom

Aldeen Davis

MUSCATINE, IOWA

ࣿ

Aldeen Davis is eighty and has lived in Iowa all her life. She has four daughters; another has passed away. She has nineteen grandchildren.

She was a local newspaper columnist for twelve years.

"I wrote about the connection between black history and today's history," she says. "It was an educational column for all people. Not just the black race. Not just the white race. All races. We have to eradicate some of that hate. That unthinking. That uncaring. We often don't even have time to say 'Hi.'

"I live in a small town on the Mississippi River. Someone was down here from New York. When he was walking down the street in Muscatine, someone said, 'Good Morning. Hi.' This almost stopped this person from New York in his tracks. We have to get back to the fact that it is a good morning. We have to get back to 'Hi.' "

The basic theme of our life and that of many of our family's ancestors has been Christian faith and life and to be of service to family and community. The oft used, if true, "leaving the world better than we found it" could be continued as a goal but one that cannot really be measured.

This includes the maximum practice in the promotion of human rights, racial blindness, and interest in people.

Ruth and Luther
Gruenbaum
ST. LOUIS, MISSOURI

If I had to write a note to my children's children and put it on the sugar bowl (which we always had on the kitchen table with Rockwood Cocoa), I would say, Stay as good as you are. Be kind and respectful.

Angelina Bertoni
FRANKLIN, MASSACHUSETTS

Forgiveness

To My Children, My Grandchildren, My Posterity for Generations to Come.

I've tried to live my life as an example to others. I've tried to raise my children to be good people. I've tried to be a good person myself. I've tried to be a good wife. But I've made some mistakes. I'm not perfect.

If there's one thing I've learned in this life, it's that you have to be forgiving of others, as well as forgiving of yourself. If you can't forgive yourself, how can you expect others to forgive you?

Live each day to the fullest and with great joy! Don't brood over hard times; I've done that at times and I can tell you that it doesn't do anyone any good.

Watch the simple things in life. Don't be too busy to watch a sunrise or a sunset. Watch a mother bird feed her babies in the nest. Spend time watching an ant colony bury its dead.

More importantly, share these things with your children! While you share these things with them, watch your children—see their faces light up when they discover that ice cream melts when exposed to heat. Watch their eyes as they pet a new puppy. Be there when they take their first steps, and when they drive a car for the first time. Don't miss a moment of their growing-up years.

Teach them to pray.

Listen to them when they talk to you.

Laurie E. White
SACRAMENTO, CALIFORNIA

Remain close to God by keeping in touch with His word. Honor your family by loving and supporting each other both in sad and happy times. Forgive each other. Reach out to help those people around you who are in need.

Gilbert Reinkensmeyer
KALAMAZOO, MICHIGAN

It is a job to carry around the burden of hatred, of self-recrimination and regret. Forgiveness does not entail a disregard for having been wronged.

Feel what you must feel, deal what you must deal. Forgiveness is a willingness to give all that a rest.

Give a gift to yourself. Erect a wall; you on one side, hatred on the other. And while you're at it, forgive your own trespasses as well.

Note to my children and all children everywhere:
Remember that God is within you and will come to

your rescue when you are in need. You must be receptive and obedient to the answers when they arrive.

Always remember to keep your thoughts positive no matter what you are going through. You can change a situation by the way you think about it.

When dealing with people, remember there is only one relationship. That is between you and God. You can always go to Him and tell Him your troubles. He loves you and always will. The way He relates to us is the way we are to relate to one another: with unconditional love.

We all mess up, but so what?

Forgive yourself first, then the other person. See what you have learned from the experience and file it in your memory bank.

Michele Grimes
CHICAGO, ILLINOIS

Remember, love conquers all, and forgiveness is an antidote that cannot be bought at a drugstore.

Donna Shankland
VALPARAISO, INDIANA

Home and Community

Last year we purchased a small farm with several barns and outbuildings on the land way west of busy Chicago. There is a grove of black walnut trees in the back and large maples lining the long driveway. The house was originally built in the mid-1800s and is typical of the large homes which raised many children.

During this year we have been fixing up the house with bathrooms, kitchen and decorating but keeping the original charm and antiquity the building originally possessed. We have been planning to fill the penned area with sheep and the chicken coop with layers and roasters ever since last summer. Finally, the time has come to where we feel comfortable enough with the land and our knowledge of raising animals that we are ready to bring them home to live with us and be part of our extended family.

The farmhouse raised several families in its lifetime and now we are tenderly giving it our time, devotion and love. The place deserves tenderness and we are now its caretakers. We owe it to the place to treat it kindly and fill it with living things that bring life to any farm.

This is a serene lifestyle which we find a very pleasant contrast from the busy, stressful lives we lived in years past. We wish everyone could be so comforted getting back to the basics.

Jan Sofranko
MALTA, ILLINOIS

Family is our first community. It is a self-contained village surrounded by four walls. The walls of our home form the place where one world stops and another begins, within.

On the inside of those walls we hang pictures of our family members. On the other side, our home meets the community—our family shares a wall with the world at large.

We are usually not the first family who has lived where we live. We are temporary settlers tied in continuity with all who dwelled here before us, and those future tenants down the line.

We can make our homes our own and we can share the good we have there. We can throw the windows open and let fresh air circulate a bit.

Just as our family extends with aunts and uncles and cousins, we have the option to open our arms to the wider world.

To the biggest neighborhood. We come, we stay, we move on.

For the past thirty years I have periodically left notes on a kitchen table. More accurately, stuck to the front door, posted on the fridge or stuck under the kitchen sink. As the spouse of a minister, and because of the nature of the beast, we have lived in many a parsonage or manse. The parsonage, for those of you who do not know, is a church-owned and cared-for home for the minister of the congregation. A manse is the same thing.

A week after annual conference is over is the time appointed and designated by our presiding bishop as "moving day." In our conference every minister moves on the same day.

It is not unusual for one family to have their last breakfast in the morning in their home and by the dinner hour another "parsonage" family will be occupying the dining room. In any event, it is common for both those meals to be eaten in the midst of moving boxes, crying children, harried spouses and curious church members who can't wait until the next Sunday for the "first look at the new preacher and his family."

To say that this is an emotional time for a parsonage family is an understatement. It doesn't make any difference what the circumstances of the move are, it is hard to do. I've received notes and left some. Most of the time they were about things like when the trash is picked up, how many appliances of the 1990s can be plugged into the 1940s wiring before sparks fly, where the best plumber, electrician and butcher are, what the schools are like, who in the church you can tell your most intimate secrets to (or who *not* to tell them to), what appliances are on their last leg, or who gave what furniture to the house to be used until it falls apart, finally. A lot of times notes will include who is in the hospital that the minister must visit the "first thing in the morning."

But it is the unseen messages that often mean the most. The ones not written with pen, but by the lives of the people who resided there.

It is the unpracticed hand of a child scrawled inside a closet that says, "My brother is so mean."

Or the mark that measures the height of a daughter on the edge of her door frame, put there the day she moved and left her friends of five years.

Or those inevitable scratches that are left on furniture no matter how hard you tried to remove them.

Or the smudges that growing sons leave jumping to touch the top of the door, smudges that you cannot bring yourself to wash off, no matter how clean you wish to leave the house.

It is the holes the dog dug, or the grave of that beloved pet beside the fence in the far corner of the backyard. It is the kitchen herb garden planted beside the door or patio. It may be one left by the former residents of the house or one you planted yourself.

Very often it's the places worn on the carpet when a child was colicky or ill. Or paced upon by parents whose teens are late. It is the late-night counseling session in the living room when someone is feeling as if life is no longer meaningful. It is the phone that rings with good news or bad news from the congregation. Or just Miss Clara who wants to tell you how much she loves you and your family and how glad she is that you reside in that house.

The notes are cups of coffee shared over the kitchen table on a sunny summer morning. Or the struggle with a homework assignment. They are the laughter of children, either yours or members of your congregation's, who think you tell the funniest stories or wear the neatest ties.

The notes are beautiful threads of the well-worn tapestry of living.

They are long business sessions, staff meetings, bazaars, mission trips, youth camp and tea with the Ladies' Society.

They are loneliness, then words of comfort, from those sainted people who take you under their wings. The ones you turn to when you are not convenient to your own family.

They are loud discussions of philosophy, theology and psychology when your family gathers on holidays around a table—discussions that are shared most of the time only by you and your spouse after your children are grown.

They are the time your family grows to include sons- and daughters-in-law and your children's children. The notes resonate as family secrets are told and memories shared.

These are the notes left on my kitchen table. They often

contain words of advice about how soon to return for a visit, how to have an effective ministry in that place, or who can or cannot do this or that in the church.

Marion Snider, pianist, gospel-song writer and dear friend, observes, "All over the world if you enter places of worship you can find hymnals with corners turned down. In the great cathedrals of Europe and in the brush arbors, people mark the hymns that are a source of strength as people go about their days. There is a commonality among the songs they choose."

Marion wrote a song, "I've Got the Corners Turned Down," about those common hymns.

Notes left on the parsonage kitchen tables throughout this nation are a lot like those hymns. There is a common thread that binds the lives of those who leave the notes. It is the "assurance of things hoped for, the evidence of things not seen."

Sandra Smith Irish
Bridgeport, Texas

෨෨

Sandra Smith Irish is fifty-two, married to a minister, and is the mother of three children. She was born and raised in Arkansas, but has been living in North Central Texas for the past thirty-two years. The longest she's lived in one place is six years; the shortest is one year.

"Most people, eventually, have a place they live that's their own. That's one thing I found in the ministry. We'll live in a church-owned home of some sort until we retire. You don't have any roots for your children. So you have to make those roots and it has to be more than the brick-and-mortar type of thing.

"Even when I thought I wasn't listening as a child, my grandmother was telling me stories," she says.

What we all have, in the end, are the stories. Our stories keep us alive.

I decided to write my stories and leave them to you. However, I couldn't prop the note against the sugar bowl. No sugar bowl now-a-days, but maybe a silk flower arrangement would grace the center of the table. Mother's and Grandmother's table would hold a rather large sugar bowl, a cut glass spoon holder with various size spoons, a butter knife, salt and pepper shakers, a vinegar cruet and empty cream pitcher. All this was covered between meals by a square of white embroidered cloth edged with fancy crocheting.

Kay Greene
Signal Mountain, Tennessee

I have found that if you treat your family members like very important friends, you and they will be so much happier.

Mary Dawn Glenn
VALPARAISO, INDIANA

Ask for Help

Remember:

The mind can fall ill, as well as the body. If you are not well in your mind, beyond a temporary fit of the blues, or an understandable grief, get help! Life is too short to spend significant parts of it in poor mental health, if it is not necessary.

> *Dora Craycraft*
> LOMBARD, ILLINOIS

To My Grandchildren,

Communicate with your parents; ask for help and advice. Remember I love you so very much.

> Grandma Angie
> *Angela Beumer*
> RAYTOWN, MISSOURI

Think of society as a customer service center, reached at no cost to you by an 800 number. There are people there to help you; people whose job it is to help you. This may not be their paying job, but the job they have taken upon themselves to do. The job of humanity—the career of loving-kindness.

No matter your problem, someone has experienced it before you and has information to provide you.

This may be a solution, or just a way to cope. A gentle voice or receptive ear.

A warm and quiet lean-to in a world of whipping wind.

Ask for help when you need help.

Provide help to others when you are able.

Remember to ask. Remember to answer.

There will come a time for both.

God, Faith and Worship

After my husband's untimely death, my son, my daughter and I had the duty of going through his bank lock box to list what he had there. Among the papers was his certificate of baptism. As we paused to read it, I felt compelled to say, "This is your most important heritage."

I now have added my certificate to the lock box and that is what I wish to leave; an affirmation of Christian faith to my children's children.

Umatilla M. Arnold
KANSAS CITY, MISSOURI

No matter how busy you are today, time spent with God should be your first priority.

Corrine Vils
MAZOMANIE, WISCONSIN

Never forget, in your daily prayers, to thank Our Lord for all of His graces and blessings.

Mary D. Siciliano
WALL, NEW JERSEY

Remember this: You are never alone. Your God, however you see Him, is always with you.

Carolyn Summers
WINNSBORO, TEXAS

Put God first in your lives and everything else will be given to you. That's what I've done and I feel peace and joy in my life.

Bonadel Purpura
NORRIDGE, ILLINOIS

Try always to let your smile and countenance reflect the real joy in your heart because you know whose child you are, no matter how old you get. Your heavenly Father is your life. Remember that and share His goodness.

Marlise Springsteen
VALPARAISO, INDIANA

One way we walk with God is as if a benevolent power is holding our hand. And in that holding of the hand, God is providing that benevolent power to us, if we are receptive to it.

Belief in God is trusting the system. It is either silence in the din or a voice in the silence, depending on our need at the time.

God can be the parent we choose. And if one considers oneself a child of God, one can then logically expect to inherit some of the Parent's traits. Then, as day follows night, as natural as spring becomes summer, a child of God will turn those traits into action, and, by example, pass those traits along again.

Beware as you proceed in this land of freedom! We travel as we please, we go and come with ease. We are at liberty to do what and when we choose. Yet man should never embark on any journey or attempt any mission without first invoking the power of God for guidance, health and strength.

Yes, there are miracles all around us every day.

Why not give God a chance?

We often bypass God entirely.

We go everywhere else for help.

We go to psychiatrists and psychologists, advisers and friends.

We take tension pills and talk-yourself-out-of-it potions.

We consult God only as a last resort.

We should run to Him at the very first symptom or sign of trouble, for God is our source of help. In Him lies the power to help, repair and redeem.

Tommie Lancaster
GRANDVIEW, MISSOURI

Do not be dismayed, for the battle is not yours, but God's.

Lois A. Dockter
MILWAUKIE, OREGON

What if God felt like the river's flow? And if you trusted, just lay back, caused no consternation, what if you let the river of God's good guidance carry you down?

Dear Ones,

It is important, as you read this, to know I am not attempting to control your lives. Each of us is responsible for own life. Change is constant; but even when you are involved in events that are out of your control, you still are in charge of your reaction and behavior toward those events.

Develop relentless honesty within yourself; even the smallest lie cracks the bedrock of your integrity. The strongest foundation you can build is one of faith. Spend some time alone each day; turn to prayer, spiritual readings or music that will strengthen the foundation for your convictions. Doing this is like money in the bank: In tough times your faith will be there to draw on.

Develop the many unique qualities given to you by God; appreciate the earth and its people; respond to these riches by giving a part of yourself in service to others. It's good to work through the conventional avenues, of course, but it is also fun to quietly do some kindness without anyone else knowing about it.

Respect the balance of body, mind and spirit. Walk in

courage and love. Reach out and grab life with both hands and experience every moment.

I love you.

Suzanne Miller Allen

ELKHORN, WISCONSIN

෨

Suzanne Miller Allen has recently married a man she's known for fifty-one years. She is sixty-six and has two children and two grandchildren.

She thinks spending some time alone every day is vital:

"Too often, we're going off into so many different directions. There is a need to have space inside ourselves, where we can know ourselves, where we can get our renewal. Even if we just retreat for a few minutes, we can recharge our batteries."

Maybe God has provided you a place to go daily with your thoughts or a house in which to worship weekly. Maybe you convene just the two of you, or in congregation with kindred souls.

To some the belief in God is so private they hardly admit it to themselves. Some are baffled and some don't even wonder.

The believers, though—all God's children— tend to want to give thanks.

Gratitude

Learn to say "Thank you," thus not take anything for granted. Thank God daily for the big things and little things in your life. Thank your parents, children, spouse, brothers and sisters, your friends for the tangibles and intangibles which weave your life together.

Helen R. Reinkensmeyer
KALAMAZOO, MICHIGAN

༺༙༻

Helen Reinkensmeyer is sixty-nine and has been married to Gilbert for forty-three years. They have three children and seven grandchildren

"As I grew up, I was taught to say 'Thank you,' " she says. "My mother grew up in a parsonage in Greece. She never returned there to see her parents alive. She was constantly saying 'Thank you.' That's what she learned to do in Greece. And she always asked me if I said 'Thank you.' Every time I say it it reminds me. Gratitude and Thank you are sisters."

Note on the Kitchen Table. What a great idea. I am seventy-seven years old and have been in bed, at home, ten months with bone cancer. What an awful thing to have. I'm going downhill fast; my four boys want me to write as much as I can. I said, Never be afraid to say "I'm sorry." If you can't be thankful for what you have, be thankful for what you escaped. A little sense of humor is very important.

Alma J. Maisel
MARTINSBURG, WEST VIRGINIA

୧୨

"My mother's note was written less than two months before her death, at a time when she was in a substantial amount of pain, but remarkably lucid," says Larry Maisel. "She remained so until about the final week of her life.

"What she said was typical of her: things I heard her say many times through the years. She kept her sense of humor until the very end, and would motion for us to come close (she had lost her voice early on) so she could tell some jokes she remembered from years before.

"One thing that I'm certain she would have included, had her mind been clearer, is 'Always think the best about people. Lord knows there are always enough people around to think the worst.'

"One final interesting fact: she predicted the day of her death nearly two weeks ahead of time, right to the day. I said, 'You don't know that.' Her reply was 'Don't be silly. Of course I do.' Obviously, she did."

Gratitude is noticing. Looking around, seeing beauty or good intent and acknowledging that you have been enhanced by it.

Noticing kindness and kismet and knowing the difference each has made in your day.

By noticing, layers of good and better moments begin to fall before you, soft white feathers floating to the ground.

Dear Family,

James 5:11, 12, 13 tells me that I know where I'll spend all of eternity and I want you to follow me there so I can meet and really know each one of you. I know we'll have a great reunion in Heaven when it comes time to leave this Earth. What a day that will be! Please be there!

I'll be watching and waiting and know I'll love every one of you.

I want each of you to know how pleased and proud I am to be one of your ancestors.

Love to you all.
Ruth Johnson Jolly
DES MOINES, IOWA

I, Loy Clark, for all of the seventy-seven years of my life, have been grateful for the help of my family and friends. I am thankful for a good home, as well as good health. I am also thankful for my ability to prosper. I have taken the ups and downs as they came. I enjoyed fishing, traveling and restoring antique cars. I want to give thanks to all.

Loy Clark
BEAVERTON, OREGON

Love and Be Loved

Here is a piece written by a brother of mine which I would like to leave in the kitchen taped to the refrigerator door.

"Rekindle the love in my heart that I may pass its flame and its warmth to others in the cold." —C. V. Pedroche

Dr. Jose V. Pedroche
LOS ANGELES, CALIFORNIA

You asked if I were to leave a note propped on my kitchen table for future generations what would it say. I would make the note brief, but meaningful; gentle, but potent; operative, but not overpowering. This is what it would say:

Life is short, but full of simple pleasures that can be the most rewarding. Make time to experience and enjoy them. You will never get those moments back. Love, and allow yourself to be loved. Every human on this earth has worth, and needs other humans to be fulfilled.

Polly Hartranft
TOLEDO, OHIO

A Note to Be Left on My Kitchen Table for My Family:

I wish everyone on this Earth could have the love and caring that I have received from my family, and could have had the blessings of God I have had to help me through the rough spots in life.

"Pretty is as pretty does." This applies to actions you all have to meet, too. Bye-bye, my precious family. I will see you in the hereafter.

> Grandma Dale
> *Dale Fyke Krohn*
> VALPARAISO, FLORIDA

∾

Dale Krohn is eighty-seven, and recently moved to Florida from Oregon. In Oregon, she often won ribbons at the fair for the dahlias from her garden. She is now living in a house across the street from her youngest son.

Can a person see love? Yes, through another's eyes. Can a person feel love? Yes, through another's arms. Can a person hear love? Yes, when another is listening.

Love is who you call to say something went

wrong. Love is who you call to say something went right. Love is that voice on the end of the phone that knows before you say it.

Love sits in the living room. Love takes your temperature when you are sick. Love takes the dog out for a walk when it is raining.

Love waits at the airport. Love will drive you home.

Love is the most tangible of all the intangibles. Love is both adhesive and air.

In the beginning, love makes us senseless. In the end, love is the only thing that makes any sense. Love involves every sense.

Can a person see love? Can a person feel love? Can a person hear love?

If you say yes, you're blessed.

Dear Ones,

Here are some final thoughts. Try to resolve differences. Don't let hatred fester. Find a partner in life and stick together like I did. Would I have ten kids again if I had the chance? You bet. I loved being Mom.

Barbara Krainock
POWAY, CALIFORNIA

Barbara Krainock, sixty-five, is mother of ten, grand-mother of eight, married nearly forty-four years to Joe, a physi-cal education teacher and coach. Barbara and Joe met when he was in the Marine Corps during the Korean War.

"Don't go to bed mad," she says.

"Finding a partner and sticking together? You've got to know Joe.

"If I had something up my craw, I'd write a letter. If I felt the same way in the morning, I'd give it to him. If not, I tore it up. Usually I tore it up. We always kiss good night. We never say goodbye without a peck on the cheek."

This is meant to be my words of wisdom to you—my children and their children. It is really very simple. Hanging above my desk is a sign.

"Those places in our personalities where we tend to de-viate from love are not our faults but our wounds."

I have one other reminder in my house. It also hung in my office for many years.

"Only one life that soon will pass. What's done with love will truly last."

Each experience in my sixty-plus years has brought me where I am today. That is the process of living. There have been good times, there have been bad times. But now there is an inner peace which I don't remember ever having felt before. Each day is full—no worries, no debts, no unfulfilled desires. I have confidence in you—my daughters and grand-children. I have loved and been loved.

Grandma

Pat Inglis

MAGALIA, CALIFORNIA

All I would say for all to know is:

The key is love!

Judith Hurta

EMBARRASS, WISCONSIN

To my family—husband and five children—genuinely, deeply!

I tried my best with what I had and what I came from.

Please forgive me for not being perfect and for having faults.

But remember, also, I chose my mate, an introverted, ethical, honest, moral, good man, to balance my extroverted, enthusiastic, artistic nature and to pass on the best to those I loved the most.

I chose mothering because it was my profession: to improve life's cycle. My family was my career. I know you're better than I was, thank God!

Geri Bishop Davison
KIRKWOOD, MISSOURI

Say It

Dear Children,

My one big regret in life is the fact I never really said anything meaningful to you. Every time I hear someone say, "My father always said . . . My mother always said . . ." I wished I heard one of you say, "My father always said . . ."

Curt Davison
KIRKWOOD, MISSOURI

෨෧

"I think I've said meaningful things, but no one, big meaningful thing," Curt Davison says. "My own parents were more action than words. Same with me.

"Our five children turned out fine, which is important. I must be doing something right."

Choose your words wisely in praise and anger, they will surely come back to you someday.

Madeline Spurck
BLUE ISLAND, ILLINOIS

A belief, stated earnestly, endures.

We have all, at times, suffered with a lack of words, or unfortunate access to the wrong ones. At times we find ourselves sputtering in that lack's aftermath, like post-ignition in an automobile.

What we'd like to do is to stand proudly, having said what needed saying in a fairly artful manner or having left alone that which should have been left alone.

Choosing the message. Broadcasting clearly.

Being rational where needed and adding pomp and circumstance at the right times.

What a release to have said what you meant, and to feel, having said it, what a bird must feel at the moment it lifts its wings and flies.

To whoever might read this:

Perhaps the most annoying problem in my life has been an innate diffidence. I stand back when I should be going forward. My life has been very good, but it could have been better. I have passed up many opportunities simply because I have been too shy to do otherwise. Where does this inability to wrestle with the world come from? I am well educated, attractive, polite and able to work out logical conclusions.

I should have been able to approach life in a more positive, adversarial manner. The time I went from Chicago to Paola, Kansas, on a train and never once got up to go to the rest room is a good example. Someone might notice me. On up to college where I did poorly on a tryout for the thespian club simply because I was so embarrassed by the person officiating. The list is endless.

Life is a banquet awaiting us, and I was too shy to approach the table.

I have come to two further thoughts:

1. I would urge readers to study *something* while they are young, and continue to study it as they grow in years. It matters not what the subject might be. It can be something quite small, but the years take a steady toll on us, and we can reach our mature years without a single area of expertise. There should be something you are expert in, and if you are, chances are you will be recognized one way or the other. Or if you are not, the good inside feeling that you know more about something than anybody else will suffice.

2. Have people to dinner. Do not be paralyzed by how you cook, nor how your dining accoutrements stack up. Simply have friends over. They care not how you keep your house, nor if the food is first-class. At one time we had numerous business friends to dinner on a weekly basis and it was no great thing to me. Then circumstances changed and slowly paralysis set in. It became a chore—always getting out the good china and buying flowers and making sure every dish was something special. I no longer enjoyed it and gradu-

ally stopped. What a shame. I lost the comradeship of count-
less people. Set your goals realistically and simply do it.

Now this should suffice.

My song is sung.

Betty Hodges

Mission, Kansas

If you would have asked me to write this note six
months ago, it would have been some funny little writing to
make you laugh. It would have made you smile at the time,
but then you would have forgotten about it.

Mom died about four months ago and since then I've
read every book I can about the afterlife, wondering if she's
still around me, if she knows how much I really, really loved
her. I will always remember her kindness, the way she loved
to tell tall stories—exaggeration was an understatement—and
how much she loved our family.

You know you take for granted the people who mean the
most to you, thinking they will always be there for guidance,
support and acceptance. Then one day, when you least expect it, you get a call and your whole life changes forever. I
find I don't cry as much as I used to. It must be part of the
healing process. But that doesn't mean I don't think of her
daily. I want to believe our loved ones are still around us,
watching us, helping us along in our destiny.

I guess the thing in life that I've learned is to always
speak from the heart. Don't leave things unsaid. If you truly

love someone with all your heart, let them know so you never have any regrets.

My biggest hope is that I have touched a life or made some kind of impression on someone out there and they will remember me.

We travel through this life but once. Let's make it count.

JoAnne Matinrazm
WINDERMERE, FLORIDA

I am proud of my children, as they have become caring, independent adults raising smart and talented grandchildren in the often difficult world of today. I have been remiss in their adult lives in telling them how much I love them and what a great job they are doing. Maybe I just hoped they could read my mind; they always said I could read theirs when they were small. (If I could read minds, I would know who broke the blue vase on the coffee table all those years ago.)

My daughter-in-law, Karen, has been a delightful addition to our family. Her love and friendship have meant a great deal to all of us, and she has been a good wife and mother. Dick, our son-in-law, is the most patient and caring young man in any family. He has driven many miles to see that we spent Christmas together as a family, and I know this hasn't always been easy. We have been blessed and I couldn't have done better if I had picked these two myself.

I hope when my children's children are reading this they

will smile and remember Grandma and how much she loves them. I want them to know that friends and family are important no matter what they decide to do in life—and I want for them always to "Remember who you are."

Marilynn Cunningham
RAYTOWN, MISSOURI

❧

"I got 'Remember who you are' from my high school principal," Marilynn Cunningham, sixty-six, says. "It was our school motto. It meant, Everywhere you go, you represent your home, your school, your town. We're just getting ready for our fiftieth year high school reunion. I'll bet that 'Remember who you are' stuck with a lot of people."

Always tell your loved ones how much you love them and how meaningless your life would be without them. I am a widow and I've wished so many times that I had told my husband how much I loved him and what life would be without him.

Loiseen Brewer
WATERLOO, INDIANA

＊

Loiseen Brewer is seventy-two and was married for forty-one years. She has lived all her adult life in the town where she was born. She has three children and five grandchildren.

"When my husband was diagnosed with a diseased heart, we knew he didn't have very long," she says. "He lived three years, but the way I handled it was to act as if it wasn't happening. I went about my business. I was never demonstrative. I wished I had stopped and hugged him, but, like I say, I'm just not that type.

"Sometimes when you're young, raising a family and paying bills, sometimes you don't want the humor. But as a senior citizen, you can see that it's good for you.

"I was sort of an introvert. My husband was an extrovert. We were good for one another. He would have been a wonderful person to grow old with. He was lots of fun."

Family life can be too real at times. The nearness and the intimacy almost beg some distance. We don't always speak about, or even see, who is next to us on the couch.

While your house is being painted, all you can

117

see are the ladders, all you can smell is the paint smell, all you can think about is that dream day in the future when the tarps get picked up and put away.

And on that day, you can cross the street and look at your house from a distance. It is as if the version of your house that you carry in your mind got a new coat of paint as well.

Sometimes, when things get too real, you can cross the street. If it is too hard to see who is sitting next to you, you can allow yourself a little distance.

Then say it, when you're ready, say it. Say all you're grateful for, say that you love, say all that is good about this day.

You won't be sorry if you say it. You'll only be sorry if you don't.

Words work.

Our World

My life took a very long time to help me to realize that one day at a time is genuinely how to live. In just one day, I could wake up, see my world for what it is, experience the freshness of the earth—flowers, trees, mountains, streams—and see the true colors shown in so much beauty.

Janet Greene
ALBUQUERQUE, NEW MEXICO

If twice a day—just twice a day—we could each step outside and breathe deeply. If each one of us could watch the way blades of grass waltz together, see the ever new surprise of pink flowers on green bushes.

If we could let the mist off the quiet water cool our soul. If only we could ignore—twice a day—all the bustle and brouhaha and listen to the calm wind.

Walking out the door is the way. Looking skyward. Outward. Feeling the returning sun on your face with your eyes closed in the morning and with your eyes open in the afternoon. Seeing how night truly does drop and fall.

Dear Ones:

Always be kind to one another and to all living things.
>Love, Ma
>*Janet Pinckney*
>BREVARD, NORTH CAROLINA

Dear Future:

1. Keep your feet dry!
2. Work hard.
3. Play hard.
4. Sleep hard.
   (Note Order)
5. Share your accumulated goods and wealth with love.
6. Share yourself with your family.
>*Harold Meyer*
>FARGO, NORTH DAKOTA

∽

Harold Meyer wrote his note before the North Dakota floods in 1997, and says he can't tell you why he put "Keep your feet dry" first on his list. He is eighty.

To My Children, Grandchildren and Other Descendants,

I would like you to truly believe that to have a wise, happy and rewarding life is one of life's greatest achievements. These simple ideas evolved in my mind over more than seventy years of living.

When I was a boy, ingrained in me mostly by my mother was belief in God, being active in church, being honest, being thoughtful and helpful to others, enjoying life and being thankful for the many good things that came my way. Before each meal and at every bedtime she had me say prayers that she had taught me.

My father's major emphasis was on more secular things such as:

Be responsible. (You are responsible for everything that you do, or that you fail to do if you should do.)

Do not be wasteful. (Practice conservation.)

Be self-sufficient and self-reliant.

Be punctual. (Be on time, but being unnecessarily early is a waste of time.)

Be trustworthy.

Be constructive and not destructive.

Be patriotic in support of your country.

All of the things I have mentioned were mutual attitudes of both my parents, but Mother dominated in some, while Father was more obvious in others.

While I was still in my youth, a strong sense of the difference between "right" and "wrong" was impressed upon me. It became clear to me that being honest included: Do not lie. Do not cheat. Give full measure. Be trustworthy.

According to my father this trustworthiness meant: Keep your promises. If you borrow something, be sure to return it without undue delay. If you use things belonging to others, put them back in exactly the same place and condition as they were when you took them.

Other emphasis by Father was in the area of conservation: that is, Do not be wasteful. Don't waste food. Clean your plate. Do not take more than you will eat. Don't waste time.

Father, while having only an eighth-grade education, also was a stickler on financial matters.

I can hear him say, "Be thrifty; pay your own way, live within your means, do not sponge on others, don't borrow money unless you can see a way to repay it. Save money to pay for your old age and take good care of your family." These were oft repeated axioms in our home.

Also heard at times were: "Work hard and play wisely"; "Give generously within your means for worthy causes"; and "Do not be stingy."

In later years, after youth, I had the privilege of learning much from many teachers and fellow workers. I had the good fortune during more than half my life to be closely associated with a great man—C. Maxwell Stanley—who was demanding and difficult but from whom I developed ideas in business that I thought were good.

Some of these were: Give credit where credit is due. Always avoid conflicts of interest. Choose friends carefully. Do not be afraid to take risks after having analytically thought through the routes to success.

Make things better for people and you will be worthy of the same.

Dear children, and those who follow you, I wish you all a wise, happy and rewarding life.

Sanford K. Fosholt
MUSCATINE, IOWA

ॳॴ

Sanford Fosholt is eighty-two and grew up on a farm in northern Iowa. First he was a farmer, and then went on to become an engineer.

"I think it's only natural that you're inclined to try to convey to your own children things from your own childhood," he says. *"Some people laugh at that one about putting things back, but I don't think it's ridiculous. I think it's sensible."*

To Whom It May Concern:

As soon as you have reached the age of reason and have come to the place where you can think for yourself, do the following:

1. Clear your mind of everything that you have believed or may have been taught about creation, religion, church and the existence of a God.
2. Try to think through what you decide to believe about these things without any outside influence upon you.
2. Live your life accordingly.

Richard A. Busemeyer
BOCA RATON, FLORIDA

To My Readers:

Perfectionism and procrastination don't get the job done to completion or even get it to a starting place.

Earl Derks
KANSAS CITY, MISSOURI

If I had to write a note, one note, and prop it up against the sugar bowl for future generations to read, it would say, Never ever own a credit card. Never charge anything. Save until you can buy that car, that new coat, those purple shoes, those diamond earrings.

Evelyn Krysl
EUGENE, OREGON

Evelyn Krysl is eighty-two and has been a beautician for more than sixty years. Her shop is attached to her house. Her daughter is a poet and teaches college.

"I don't have a credit card," Evelyn Krysl says. "If I can't afford it, I don't get it. People can get along without so many things. My husband was a music teacher. We always had a house. We had enough to make a down payment, then we'd sell that one and put a down payment on another one."

Platitudes and pronouncements don't make the world go round. Except that maybe they do.

Maybe the major issues they melodiously convey are the unseen currents that keep the whole thing twirling.

Between each major issue and the next, though, are a multitude of cogs and gears that require attention. These are the "Measure Twice, Cut Onces" of life; the "Right Is Tight" rule of turning screws.

These are the things we either find out by doing, or learn because someone is kind enough to take the time to show us the shortcut step.

The way a father will describe the vagaries of

taxes by moving piles of pennies. The way we learn to pack luggage correctly or set the table. Somebody showing us, for the first time, how to pump gas.

Advice for my grandchildren: Work diligently in school. Develop good habits at home, in school and at work. Pick out congenial friends with whom you can share common interests. Save part of your income in preparation for retirement.

Rodney Shankland
VALPARAISO, INDIANA

Listen up, Posterity:

Very few things in life are totally black or white; most of the information upon which we are forced to make decisions falls somewhere in the gray area in between.

We are, of course, really not allowed that option in our personal life or in family matters. Prayerful deliberation would seem to be the best course in cases of this kind.

How about our public life? How do we decide whom to vote for or what our opinions should be on issues that make their way onto the ballot or are being discussed with great emotion by those with whom we come in contact?

A dialogue with those whose opinions we trust can be helpful, but we are mostly dependent on the print and broadcast media for information. I lean toward the printed page; most newspapers present a fairly well-balanced view through their editorials, outside columnists and letters to the editor.

The broadcast media can be helpful; public radio and TV do a good job. Paid political advertisements should, I believe, be ignored completely as the frequency with which they are shown is generally directly proportional to the amount of special-interest money going into the campaign, and the short commercials are designed to appeal to the emotions and not the intellect of the viewer.

Claire L. Smith
MUSCATINE, IOWA

The great secret success formula for all time is:
Listen
Observe (keenly)
Manners
Beat yesterday

Roger Egerton
WEATHERFORD, OKLAHOMA

As you live your life, identify your gifts and use them frequently or you will lose them.

Vivian Templin
CINCINNATI, OHIO

My story (I am writing it to my three children) starts in 1924 in Sioux City, Iowa, and how I wish I had kept journals down through the years. Like many folks, my memory is not much to brag on, so the one thing I try to impress in my children and grandchildren is, keep journals! Keep a record. Your children and their children's children will be forever grateful.

For the note on the kitchen table, my wife said she would probably leave a single word—"Adapt." Mine would probably be two words—"Be responsible."

William Rhodes
FREDERICKSBURG, VIRGINIA

Reading and Learning

Educate yourself through travel, books and the magic of the world.

Marian Moore
BOWLING GREEN, OHIO

As you grow up, school is one of the greatest influences in your life. Absorb all you can for as long as you can and don't worry too much about grades. Once you're grown, you'll be the sum total of all your experiences and knowledge you've gained—no one will care very much about what grades you got. Learning should and can continue all your life, and not just in the classroom. Reading truly is the key to all learning and something you can do all your life.

Everyone learns at a different pace and not everyone is interested in the same things. Not everyone does well in school, but we all find our niche in life eventually.

William E. Bennett
ELGIN, ILLINOIS

William Bennett is fifty years old, has been married for twenty-two years and has lived in Illinois all his life.

"School is a very large part of a person's life," he says. "It affects every part of your life. I see it every day."

If the appreciation of nature is found by going outward, the enjoyment of reading is found by going inward and discovering all the worlds available to us there. Through a book, we can spend time anywhere, can see anything and feel everything.

Our minds are accordion files that expand to include everything we choose to learn. We can add knowledge all our life, and the mind will expand to fit it all in, like forgiving Levi's.

When children learn to read they are given a lifetime of both travel and repose. They learn to enter their own quiet spaces through pages, to recognize that their minds are not only files, but accordions that can play a joyful polka, that they are all magicians and scholars and wise.

They can be kept company, they can be guided, they can follow trails and dig deep and breathe ideas. They can enter in fragments and emerge whole.

What a gift, what a creation—for the children—just the alphabet and reading.

All they need is love and a library card. The world is theirs.

Dear Kids,

If I don't return soon, I know you'll take care of things here.

Please remember first that integrity is everything. Then take advantage of every opportunity to better yourselves intellectually and financially.

Keep reading.

Keep writing.

Keep asking questions.

Learn from mistakes.

Do your best to make wise decisions, because "of all sad words of tongue or pen, The saddest are these: 'It might have been.'"

Enjoy life.

With love,

Mom

Orma Schmidt
MUSCATINE, IOWA

Dear Family,

I have no way of knowing whether you will be reading my message in the near future or in the distant future, so I do not know how familiar you will be with who I am. What is the message I would like to leave for you?

Simple.

Love one another.

Be true to yourself.

Take your education seriously. It is your future.

You can be anything you want to be.

Never stop learning. The brain truly starts to rust when you stop using it.

The only limits in life are those you place on yourself.

Believe in God, whether you find Him in church, a synagogue or in the great outdoors.

Follow the Golden Rule: Treat others as you wish them to treat you.

Don't spend time looking for happiness. It looks for you.

Seek peace, contentment and fulfillment. They are lasting.

Be especially kind to old people and animals.

Believe in angels.

Marianne T. Holmer
OGDEN DUNES, INDIANA

Marianne Holmer has been a Hoosier all her life, always living within thirty-five miles of where she grew up. She is sixty-two and has been married for forty-four years. She went back to college at fifty. At fifty-nine, she got a degree in management, and will go for her master's degree next.

"I think we have three ages," she says. "Childhood, adulthood and then the third age, where we have options."

A note I would leave for those who come after me:

Be kind to others, but especially be kind to yourself. You have all sorts of potential. Discover and use the power in yourself. Don't feel you have the strengths of others, use those you do have and learn from the others. Above all, learn to laugh and laugh at yourself.

Lucille Torhan
MERRILLVILLE, INDIANA

Ain't Easy

It does you no good to grow bitter
When life up and hands you a slam.
Lie down and you're marked as a quitter.
Just grit your teeth and say "Damn!"

My mother's saying!
Connie Davis
CENTRALIA, WASHINGTON

It's the journey there, not the arrival. Never give up, accept defeat and go forward.
Mary Clopton Knight
REDDING, CALIFORNIA

Life has many peaks and valleys. Love and be good to one another. The valleys will be much easier to bear and the peaks so much happier to share if there is love.
Anna Marie Coruzzi
MANHEIM, PENNSYLVANIA

Take care of yourself. Have many happy days. Remember all the good things in life. Place the bad things in your computer bank and try not to recall them. But you will never forget them.

Joseph Coruzzi
Manheim, Pennsylvania

⤳

Joseph Coruzzi, seventy-one, and Anna Coruzzi, sixty-two, have been married for forty-three years. They have two daughters and three grandchildren.

"My mother passed away when I was two," Anna Coruzzi says. "I had a very traumatic childhood. I knew that when I had my own family, the important thing I wanted to get across was love. To do everything with love. It adds to your life, and everyone else's, as well."

"I can only say I tried to make a positive statement," Joseph Coruzzi says. "Try to be positive if you can. I don't know if you always can be, but you can always try."

Survive.
Ann Pestalozzi
Murphys, California

※

"I'm from a middle-class family. I'm middle-class," Ann Pestalozzi says. "It seems strange that my one word would be 'Survive.' You might expect me to say 'Remember your table manners' or something."

She is sixty-six, has five children and nine grandchildren, and her survival instincts come from the stories she heard when she was growing up about difficulties faced by members of both sides of the family. Her grandfather was an orphan in Europe who would later fight for child labor laws. Other relatives worked for the Underground Railroad. They fled from Ku Klux Klan members who were coming after them with tar and feathers. Pestalozzi's relatives rushed out of their home in Arkansas, leaving food still cooking on the stove.

These larger-than-life family stories brought the idea of heroics to a quiet existence. And when, as a child, her mother was too ill to care for her, Ann Pestalozzi's grandfather stepped in. He provided not only the help she needed, but the kind of heroics not recorded in history books.

Into each life . . . well, you know the rest. Sometimes it rains and sometimes it floods and sometimes it seems as if tears will never stop falling. And sometimes you think that if the skies ever do clear, no flowers will grow here again.

Loss is a given. There is nothing fair about it, and axioms can at times make matters seem even worse.

But we keep walking. We climb over rocks, we stumble on pebbles, we scratch ourselves on brambles. We cower in the night.

We lose our way, we feel fear, we find ourselves at sea. Why continue when the waves threaten to bash us, when we can't tell what's next—and even if we could tell, we're not sure we're strong enough to take it?

Because our father walked. And his father before him.

The road isn't easy. Knowing this is a gift that we carry.

There are seasons, and one of the seasons is sorrow. It arrives and we're scraping the ice off the windshield when everywhere else it is spring.

Despite what you may have heard, rainbows do not always follow rain. But you will always be okay if, when you find yourself ankle-deep in mud, you can smile at the sight of cattail shoots poking through the muck beneath your feet.

Regina M. Brault
BURLINGTON, VERMONT

∽

Regina Brault lost her husband eight years ago to cancer. He was fifty-two. She is fifty-nine. When he got so sick, they moved into a house that was nearer to the hospital.

Between this house and the neighbor's house, there was a stand of willow trees. The neighbors had cut the willows down.

In the spring, while out walking, Mrs. Brault noticed that cattails had sprung up where the willows used to be. She had never noticed anything else growing there.

"I thought, 'Isn't that beautiful?' I saw something good. So I moved on. I kept going."

Dear Children,

I have learned a lot over the years. I thank God for leading me. If I had to do it over, not much change would I do.

I thank God for giving me a good husband and three lovely children and now twelve grandchildren and thirteen great-grandchildren, and this far I am in good health.

It wasn't so easy, it was hard sometimes, but God's grace and mercy brought me through.

God bless.

Cora Anderson

BEAUMONT, TEXAS

Cora Anderson is eighty-two, and came to Beaumont from Louisiana. She worked at "odds and ends" during her life. Her husband, Rodney, worked at a refinery. She was expecting twins during the Depression. Rodney was out of work. One of the twins died as a young adult. The Andersons raised three children and made certain they were educated well.

"This is what Rodney told me before he died," Cora Anderson said. "He said, 'Honey, we had a hard time but we made it.'"

Celebrate when times are hard, 'cause the good times take care of themselves.

Judy Garton
FORT WORTH, TEXAS

Path and Pattern

Dear Sandy and Misty,

I remember the days when each of you was born. They were the proudest and happiest days of my life. You two have been my greatest source of joy and the cause of my most trying times. There is so much that I want to teach you and so much that you must learn on your own. If I could pass along some "pearls of wisdom" I think it would be these:

1. First and foremost, love yourself. You cannot truly love anyone else until you love yourself. Never depend on anyone else for your happiness. Happiness is a gift that you give yourself and it must come from within.

2. Be honest and trustworthy. The world needs a lot more honest people. Deceit causes so much pain for yourself as well as others.

3. Be kind and thoughtful. A good deed may take just a moment of your time but it will probably make the day of the receiver. (It also makes you feel terrific.)

4. Don't judge other people. We are all ultimately responsible for our own actions. Accept the responsi-

bility for yours and let others accept the responsibility for theirs.

5. Keep learning. Learn something new every day. It doesn't have to be formal education—just keep your mind open every day to new thoughts and ideas. If we stop learning, we stop living.

6. Be patient and tolerant with your children. Remember, they will be learning their parenting skills from you. I wish I had been more patient with you two at times.

7. Love unconditionally. Love is the greatest gift that you can give and it should be given freely and without strings attached. Remind your spouse and your children daily that they are loved and are the most important thing in your life.

8. Be forgiving. Never hold a grudge. A grudge hurts the person holding it the most—it almost never hurts the person it is being held against. Forgiving can be the most wonderfully freeing experience.

9. Keep dreaming. Always hold on to your hopes and dreams and keep planning for the future. Half the fun of any trip is the planning and anticipating.

10. Last, but certainly not least, remember to have fun. Don't get so caught up in the struggles that you forget about the joys in life. Do something fun every day. Take the time to laugh. Life is to be enjoyed, not just endured.

Remember always that I love you both more than life

itself. Please pass that love on to your children and your children's children.

Love always, Mom

P.S. Now that you have read this note on the kitchen table, take out the trash!

Ellen Noble
RENO, NEVADA

Always—take a chance! If your head and your heart are urging you to try something, meet that challenge. The end result may not always be what you hoped, but that's fine! At least you will never go through life wondering "What if?" or "If only . . ."

Patricia Posito
CHATSWORTH, CALIFORNIA

There is no map here. This is perhaps the scariest aspect of life. Even though our parents try with all their might and would like nothing better, they are unable to predict what is going to happen, or tell us how to get there from here.

It is somehow helpful to know that our parents stumbled, too, and even though they admit the difficulty, they'd recommend the trip.

They'd throw confetti and shout *Vaya con Dios* as we waved from the deck of our journey. We could see *Bon Voyage* written on their hats as they smiled on shore.

At some point in my life I made a decision to focus on what I could do rather than on what I couldn't do. It was becoming easy to make excuses: I am too tired, too weak, too old, too poor. I don't have the knowledge. I don't have the time. I am just a woman, and women can't do these things.

I had always wanted to write a book, so I told myself, I can write a book. I didn't know how to write a biography, so I had to learn from reading and studying biographies. I was working full-time, therefore I had to make time to do my research and writing—evenings, weekends and vacations. When I began, I had no idea if or when I would find a publisher. Four years later, I held a hardback copy of my book in my hand!

To celebrate what my change of attitude had helped me accomplish, I ordered a personalized license plate for my car that read "ME-CANN." True, the letters spell out my initials and part of my name, but I chose the words deliberately for their childlike affirmation. "Me can!" Any two-year-old will say "Me do it," but somewhere in our growing up we learn to say "I can't." The can-do philosophy is not just a license to be self-indulgent and follow our whims; rather it should be used to make wise choices that we know express our true selves and to bolster our determination to follow those choices.

You, my dear grandchildren or whoever reads this note, will get mixed messages from your environment as I did. But if you are willing to work and learn, you can do and be what you feel in your heart is right for you. You can turn away from the popular messages and find your own path.

By extending this idea, regardless of our limitations, if we do what is right and what we do best, we can make a difference. Collectively, we might even contribute to solving some of the world's problems. We can if we think we can.

Marilyn E. Cannaday
LENEXA, KANSAS

ॐ

Marilyn Cannaday is sixty-five and has spent most of her life in the northeast Missouri/Kansas area. She raised four children and lost a daughter to cancer. She has six grandchildren. Her current passion is teaching older people to write.

"A little note on the kitchen table, what a better way to give advice," she says. "This way you get the last word."

I am eighty-seven years old with four grown children, seven grands and a husband who died in August 1992 after fifty-nine years of marriage. When I read the last chapter of *To Our Children's Children* I recalled a favorite clipping. It is not original, but it says it all. This could be my Note on the Kitchen Table.

*My life is a tapestry woven from many strands:
things I have done, people I have known, and places*

I have been. There is a strand for each of my dreams and aspirations since childhood. Some have been dropped in the weaving but most have simply been woven into a new design. It is a tapestry woven of light and darkness, and even in the times of greatest darkness there are strands of light which shine more brightly in contrast to the surrounding darkness.

I carry this tapestry with me always. Often I keep the past tightly rolled up—it is easier to carry that way. But I find myself now at a particular point where I want to unroll the tapestry and marvel at the patterns and designs that have been created. At different stages, different colors and textures predominate. Everything that has brought me to this point in my life is here. All of it is who I am now.

If the past and the present are here, is not the future also? Is the potential for all that I can be contained in this tapestry? I want to move forward from this point conscious of the patterns in my life and the design I am creating with it.

by Sue Kimmel

Dorothy Robinson
APPLETON, WISCONSIN

Dorothy Robinson heard Sue Kimmel's philosophy in church, and asked to get a copy of it right away. It just seemed to make sense to her, it was a philosophy she could agree with.

"I had been making braided rugs, doing handiwork," she says. "This idea of a pattern repeated, well, when you do look back, you do see that things worked out as they should. Sometimes you look back and it feels like a jumble. But when you think about it and see a pattern, it makes you feel like there's a plan."

The pattern of Dorothy Robinson's life has been one of taking things in stride. She and her husband lived in the same house for thirty years until his poor health necessitated a move to a nursing home. He passed away, and later, she had a stroke. She uses a walker now to get herself around.

When she wrote her family history, she added a chapter at the end which she called "Four Crises and How I Coped."

She gave copies to her children, and now her grandchildren have read them. She thought looking at life's hardships and the way one deals with them would be valuable knowledge for generations to come.

"The fact that I could get through these things, that's what held me together."

No experience is bad, no word is ever wasted, and though tears fall, there is a reason for every one. I'll never forget and not once will I ever regret.

Wendy Wharff
MARIETTA, OHIO

Remembering

While I don't dwell or live in the past, I do enjoy visiting with an old friend or relative and have some comment come up in our conversation that will trigger a memory of the past, or have a smell or a tune lift the veil on those memories of long ago. After all, our memories are all we really own. Material things come and go but our past belongs exclusively to us.

Gene Lowry
LAWRENCEVILLE, GEORGIA

Memories: my daydreams, a gift to myself, a video of my life, a picture of my past, my own private book of adventures, a rearview mirror into the future, or the history of yesteryears. What a treasure to have and to share with loved ones!

Shirley Felz
KANSAS CITY, MISSOURI

Shirley Felz has lived within a seventy-mile radius of Missouri all her life. She has two children, her husband has seven. Between them, they have eighteen grandchildren.

"Memories are something special I have within myself that I can pull up anytime," she says. "And I can pass my memories on to future generations. While I'm telling them my story, I'm also telling them about the history of the time. To let them see how things were in that period. Something besides just me. But memories are a gift I can give myself, too. They become your daydreams."

Our past cannot tell our future, but maybe we need not be so goal-oriented when looking back. Maybe looking back can be done for pleasure; something more involving than a magazine or HBO.

We tend to move forward and forward and forward and not take the small, free vacation of looking back.

We think we have to see the whole thing at once. We don't realize we can be archaeologists, examining layers.

Remembering when we were children, when we

were young adults, when we worked here, when we moved there.

Reflection for reflection's sake can make for an appealing afternoon of instant recall. Each life contains so many lives and loved ones. It's nice, from time to time, to revisit them all.

"It was the best of times, it was the worst of times" certainly applies to my life span as well as to the times in *A Tale of Two Cities!*

In my youth there were no gangs, no drugs and very little crime. We all had fun times just being together at homes and in church and school activities. We played games and danced to the best music of any time and saw the excellent movie musicals.

World War II was certainly a time of great concern but we were a caring nation and everyone worked together to save our country.

Gloria Palmer
GRASS VALLEY, CALIFORNIA

Imagine for a moment that you listen to senior citizens from a rural area as they reminisce about the "good old days." You may wonder just how good the "good old days" really were and just how much times have changed:

A trip was driving thirty miles away to shop, but only once or twice a year.

The fun of tipping over an outhouse on Halloween.

Trying to be good all week to get a dime allowance for the movies.

Jumping on the running board of a car for a free ride.

Receiving one toy for Christmas and being happy.

Ice and roller skates that clamped around the soles of your shoes.

Shaking cream in a fruit jar to make butter.

Safely walking three miles home because you wanted to stay in town longer than your parents on Saturday.

Never living in a house with plumbing until you were eighteen.

Friends piling in the rumble seat for a joyride.

Wearing shoes until the hole in the sole was too big for a piece of cardboard to stay inside.

Making up your own games when there was nothing to do.

Knowing that the chores had to be done before playtime.

Attending a one-room school where one teacher taught all eight grades and was also the janitor, nurse and counselor.

Realizing it was a privilege to attend school and respecting your teachers.

Learn from your experiences, both good and bad, because they make us who we are. Each person is unique, so be proud of who you are . . . and have fun along the way!

Evelyn Smith
KANSAS CITY, MISSOURI

Dear Family,

The preparation of my book *From the Beginning—According to Grandma* has been a labor of love for Dad and me. You know how Dad loves to reminisce, so you know we have had many enjoyable hours remembering the events of past years as we have gone through our many albums of pictures and boxes of memorabilia. In so doing we realized over and over how we have been richly blessed by having such a wonderful family. Perhaps this poem best expresses my wishes for each of you:

I cannot leave you riches
Nor gold and jewels—I fear—
I'll leave some small material things
And values I hold dear.

I'll look into my own heart
And see if there's something there
That is worth passing on to you
The children, in my care

I would want you to have compassion
For all God's living things—
And may you be granted patience
With your fellow human beings.

I guess there's nothing else I find
Except the things above—
But if I had to choose just one—
I would leave you love.

>   —Bette G. Wilson
>   All my love, Mom and Grandma
>   *L. Barbara Baskin*
>   KANSAS CITY, MISSOURI

To my granddaughters, Meghan and Kathleen,

Store every growing-up memory in your hearts, as one day your memories will be the treasures you can look back upon in your golden years.

>   Love always, Grandma Smalley
>   *Ruth M. Smalley*
>   ROSELLE, NEW JERSEY

∽

Ruth Smalley is seventy-five and has lived in New Jersey all her life. She has been married fifty-three years and has two sons and two granddaughters.

"I look back on my grandmother. I loved her so dearly," she says. "I think it's so important to have memories of your

grandparents from the years when you were growing up. I say to my granddaughters all the time, 'Oh, I wish you could have known my grandma.'

"And one of them said to me, 'She's rubbed off on you, Grandma.'"

Happiness and Satisfaction

I have had a long life and a good life. Have four wonderful children, eight grandchildren, three great-grandchildren.

I don't think I'd change anything one way or the other.

I've learned not to expect too much and to accept what I get with a grateful heart.

> God bless you all.
> *Ralphena J. Cameron*
> Kincaid, Illinois

∾

Ralphena Cameron is eighty-two, and was named for her grandfather, Ralph, who wanted "really badly" for her mother to have a boy. She lives in a small former mining town of eighteen hundred people and has for the past fifty years.

"I don't think I'd change," she says. "My children were very good. I had a wonderful husband. If I had to redo anything, I couldn't spot out one thing I'd like to change. Some-

times people will set their aims very, very high to get to the top of that mountain. Then when you get to the top, it's not what you expect. If you accept what comes to you every day, you'll live a more peaceful life."

Dear JR, Leslie, friends:

Don't worry, be happy. It's a philosophy I wish I'd learned earlier in life. I spent a lot of time worrying about the future, and now, in hindsight, the future took care of itself and exceeded my greatest expectations. I have found, again with hindsight, that I'm proud of my life—mistakes, follies, triumphs and simple pleasures. I became the person I wanted to be.

I was who I was—what you saw was what you got—the plain, unvarnished truth. I tried to live by the truths I held important and that wasn't always easy. I believed that the best lessons are taught by example, not by words, and I tried to live the lessons I wanted to teach.

Life offers no guarantees except that there will be rough moments, but if you face them, you will emerge bloody but unbowed. I have been the captain of my own fate as I believe we all ultimately are. I have been lucky to learn in my later years—particularly at the time of my retirement—just how many friends I actually have. That's a humbling experience and very gratifying.

My proudest accomplishment is the life of my son who

has exceeded my wildest dreams. My second proudest moments were related to teaching and the friends and family I acquired over the years are treasures that have made me realize how lucky I've been and how richly blessed.

I would hope that most people are able to look over their lives and find that the pluses outweigh the negatives. I have had a wonderful life, filled with peaks and valleys. Slowly I've learned to see some of the recurring patterns and cherish them and the quilt of my life.

Ann Booth
INDIANAPOLIS, ILLINOIS

My thoughts: I believe in being your own best friend and liking yourself. Be content with your life. Expect some hardships, strive to achieve new goals, be sensible, prudent and good to yourself. There are many paths available to all of us. Some will be just right and others will challenge you. These are the ones that make us who we are and contribute to our growth.

It's been a great journey. It's worked for me. I feel happy and fulfilled. I think happiness is often there and not recognized.

Jo Ann Lucas
WASHINGTON COURTHOUSE, OHIO

❦

Jo Ann Lucas is sixty-nine, has two sons and three grand-daughters and has lived in central Ohio for most of her life. She works in nursing and spent twenty-two years as a community care nurse.

"When I was doing this," she says, "the one thing I thought was, everybody has all these needs, but I've always been satisfied with what I had. I never had any great yearnings. I'm grateful I see things this way. So many people don't. We laugh and we say it's as if I walk around in my own comfort blanket."

What do we think happens? That we come to the end of our life, and we look back, very officially, and decide whether or not it was to our satisfaction? Do we know when that moment of judgment will be? Are we given that information?

And what if we were to come to that time and what if we answered No?

No, I was not happy. No, I was not satisfied.

By then it would be too late to change. Too late to go back and live differently so we would be able to answer Yes when we got to the end.

Yes, I was happy. Yes, I was satisfied with my life.

Now, though—today—we are in the midst of it. We have the time. Now is the place to decide.

This is your life. Why not be happy? Why not recognize the happy moments?

It doesn't have to be exuberant. It can be simply happy.

Quiet happy. Content.

If I could give you each happiness I would wrap the packages beautifully, and make them up by the dozen to pass out. But happiness and contentment cannot be given as a gift, they can only be learned and earned by our own efforts. So what I can give you is this sheet. It has the formula, the secrets of happiness—guaranteed, but you have to apply yourself to creating that life which will allow happiness to fill the crevices of your living.

Recognize your own goodness—and build on it.

Remember the house rule: you do not have the right to hurt yourself or anyone else physically, mentally, emotionally or spiritually. Live by it. When possible, help others to grow and improve their lives in each of these areas.

One line in the physician's oath by Hippocrates is "First, do no harm." This is a good philosophy to live by.

Learn from every situation, and anytime you keep running into the same problem over and over look at what you're doing to cause or attract it. We cannot prevent problems, but how we look at them and choose to handle them can make problems a building block or a stumbling block for ourselves and others. Always work on developing building blocks—and being one.

You will never find happiness by looking for it. Happiness can only come when you get outside yourself and work to make life better for others. When you concentrate on yourself, you only become more aware of your own deficiencies and how much your life lacks. Spend much time concentrating on yourself and you're heading for depression. Get outside yourself—concentrate on helping others and your life will automatically get better.

Learn, learn, learn about yourself, about your situations, about whatever you want to get involved in or are involved in. Don't whine about situations, and don't worry about them either. Learn everything you can about them, make changes to bring about the best outcome possible, and let it go. Worrying and whining can only make situations worse. They have never contributed to a better outcome.

Keep an open mind—not so open that your brains fall out, but be receptive to new ideas and concepts. Do not limit yourself to the most accepted philosophy, ideas or practices of the day. No one group, expert, philosophy, religion, doctor, etc., etc., etc., has all the answers. Many factions may each have a portion of the truth. Be open to truth wherever you may find it. (And remember, you don't have a lock on the truth either—none of us do.)

Never take yourself too seriously. No one gets out of this alive so enjoy the people and things you love while you have them. Keep a sense of humor about everything. It's an extremely rare situation that has nothing funny about it. Above all be able to laugh at yourself—you can be your own best amusement.

Develop your spirituality. You don't have to be religious to be spiritual—religion sometimes gets in the way. Your personal relationship with God can be the most stabilizing element in your life. Pray for what you need, but always pray to stay in the center of God's will, and for help adapting to that will. Pray that the doors you need to go through will be open, and that those that lead you off your path will be closed. And thank God every day for the constant stream of blessings He provides—starting with being born in the United States where an unbelievable number of options are available to each of us; where learning is available through free libraries if you can't get what you need through classes; where 95 percent of our population are within the top 10 percent of the wealthiest people on this planet; where within our family we have so much food we can be picky about what we "feel" like eating at a particular meal; where we sleep on mattresses instead of the floor, under enough blankets to keep us warm, with pillows to provide extra comfort; where we have enough excess funds to feed, house and get medical care for our pets when huge portions of the population cannot do these things for their children. Be aware of your wealth and thank God for it every day.

Above all, remember that you are loved, very dearly. You have an obligation to pass that love on to your spouse, to your children, to your extended family, and to your friends. Through passing it on, it grows, and you get much more back than you can imagine. That is what I wish for you most of all—abundant love.

Janis Jordan Hudec
ARDMORE, OKLAHOMA

෧෨

Janis Hudec is forty-eight, her son is twenty-eight and they live within a 100-mile radius of brothers and sisters and nieces and nephews.

"We're real fortunate with that," she says. "The older I get the more I appreciate the impact extended family has on raising a child. Kids really need someone significant who, when you're acting crazy, can say, 'Oh, that's just your mom today.'

"The house rule. That's the basic rule I instituted when my son was very tiny. It went from 'Tommy, you can't hit people in the head' up through hurting people with words. Hurting the

environment. It's a growing thing. Not just for my son, for myself, too."

I believe that in most situations in life you can choose to be happy or unhappy. I have chosen to be happy.

Adelaide Bogener
RAYTOWN, MISSOURI

Never take yourself too seriously!

John D. Rugg
GRANVILLE, OHIO

Laugh at spilt milk!

Barbara A. Krainock
POWAY, CALIFORNIA

Enclosed is a copy of the poem which I am leaving for my children at the time of my death.
One day my life will end; and lest
Some whim should prompt you to review it,
Let her who knows the subject best
Tell you the shortest way to do it:

Then say, "Here lies one doubly blest."
Say, "She was happy." Say, "She knew it."

—Jan Struther
Kate Hawkins
CINCINNATI, OHIO

Kate Hawkins has five children, seven grandchildren and one godchild.

"*Those lines just said it perfectly. I'm seventy-six and I think everybody who has reached that age has had tragedy of some kind,*" she says.

"*Basically, I've inherited a rather optimistic view of the human race from my mother. I am from a Quaker family who have kept journals down through the years. I've studied those and gotten attitudes of joy. The Quakers are not known as very emotional people, but somewhere in those diaries, in among all the hard work, a 'This has been a beautiful day' will pop out.*"

And, at times, the happiness goes under the surface of the water. Circumstances beyond all control flood and submerge. The very essence of hope, however, is the belief that happiness is a cork on the ocean.

It will find its way to the surface again.

H e a v e n

To My Children, Their Children and Even Their Children,

There are many things going through my mind right now that I would want to share with you. I desire that our granddaughters keep themselves pure for their future mates and that our grandsons also keep themselves for that one and only. That is the only way to guarantee a truly happy and successful marriage. This is my desire for you, but it is also God's will for you.

I want you all to know that I pray for you, by name, every day. I even pray for your future mates, and for your future children. I pray that you all will experience God's love, and that you will serve Him all your life.

This is my most heartfelt wish for all of you. It is what we taught your moms and dads, and what we believe they taught you. I love you all very much, and look forward to meeting you in Heaven someday.

Your Grandma Medema
Dolores Medema
HOMEWOOD, ILLINOIS

My Dears,

I won't say goodbye to you because I believe that we will meet again in another sphere—a land where endless peace and rapture and luminous beauty exist, beyond the power of mortals to imagine.

We are merely transients here on earth and our sojourn is as brief as the flickering light from the candles on a child's birthday cake. Measured in eternity our lives are as fleeting as the morning dew at sunrise. It is imperative that we make good use of the few moments we have to call this planet our home.

When I was a child of twelve years, I lived within a short bicycle ride of a large and attractive cemetery that had an inviting gazebo on its grounds. I often pedaled to that quiet spot to write and read the inscriptions on the tombstones.

One inscription impressed me more than all the others I had read. The words seemed profound to me. This is what I saw, etched on a stone: "Character survives, goodness lives and love is immortal." I sensed, even as a child, that this was an important message, and it remained in my memory throughout my life. Years later, I discovered who had written it. It was part of Robert Ingersoll's tribute to his brother who had died.

I have many human frailties and faults, but through the

years, as I matured and learned from my mistakes and sage advice from my elders, I strove to attain those noble virtues that Ingersoll's brother must have possessed.

Shakespeare wrote that the world is a stage and each person in it plays many parts. In playing mine I cannot know if I have attained those lofty goals that first inspired me when I was a child. Only an infinite God can answer that awesome question. All I can say is that I have tried, to the best of my finite ability, to build a decent character, a goodness of heart and to love my fellow man and the creatures of the Earth.

My beloved friends and kinsmen, may all your character survive, your goodness live and may your love become immortal.

> God bless you till we meet again.
> Yours in Eternity.
> *Nancy Niemeyer Graham*
> RAYTOWN, MISSOURI

∾

Nancy Niemeyer Graham is sixty-eight and has one son, three grandchildren and one great-granddaughter. "I was very fortunate," she says. "I had parents who were interested in literature and the arts. I was read to since I was born. I learned to read before I went to school. I wish every child could be that lucky.

"I have always believed in immortality. What good we've done, our love for each other, lives on."

Heaven—and we can only imagine—must feel like that singular relief of your own key in your own lock at day's end. For Heaven is available inside our own doors. And if all that glory is there for the taking in this life, who can blame us for expecting even more in the next?

This Earth is both our garden and our burial ground. To make our leave-taking even imaginable, we think about moving to another town, a town where all our loved ones live right down the street.

They are waiting for us on their front porches in their robes and slippers. Our old dogs are waiting with them, tails wagging just as we recall.

Some of us are sure of this. Some of us are hopeful. Some have booked nonrefundable tickets. All of us would love to see the brochure.

But that is then, and this is now, and we're back to making our own Heaven. We put our own key in our own lock in our own door.

And if there is not someone there waiting, at least maybe there's a note on the kitchen table.

My sisters and I are writing the memories of our ninety-one-year-old mother. I would like to share her note to leave in the kitchen, propped up against the sugar bowl:

I love you all very much and hope to have you all with me again someday in Heaven.

Ellen Lynn
TOPEKA, KANSAS

Heaven is a place where you will look down at Earth and see only the good things.

Joseph C. Coruzzi
MANHEIM, PENNSYLVANIA

Lastly

Dearly Beloved Children to Come,

This is your turn, have a whirl!

Embrace your life with joy and enthusiasm. Love and cherish all living creatures who share this time and this space with you.

Oh children, delight in your days. May you be blessed and be a blessing to others all your life long.

Judy Grace Stetson
FALMOUTH, MASSACHUSETTS

৩৩

Judy Grace Stetson is sixty and married to an oceanographer. She lived in Cambridge before moving to Falmouth. She has two children and one "pumpkin of a grandson."

"I have a Quaker aunt and uncle," she says. "I believe in peace and justice and I firmly believe that you cannot have peace if you do not have justice. And I believe that this is your

time. This is your place. To have the joy. To do the good. Now is when you're joyful and accountable."

If I had to write a note—one note—and leave it propped against the sugar bowl on my kitchen table for future generations, it would read:

Love does not die.

Larry A. Barnes
OCALA, FLORIDA

Walk with God, enjoy life, care for others and the world you live in, develop the full potential of your body, mind and soul.

Clara A. Olivas
ALBUQUERQUE, NEW MEXICO

It has often crossed my mind, during troubled times, how comforting, could I see a note from my mother on my kitchen table. It would be a favorite piece by Robert Browning which she quoted so often to her children.

"God's in His Heaven—All's right with the world."

Margaret Lev
ARLINGTON HEIGHTS, ILLINOIS

As to what one note I would leave on the kitchen table for my children's children, that's easy:

The food's in the fridge.

Robert W. DeBuhr
RAINIER, OREGON

To Our Readers

We'd like to ask you yet another question. We're wondering if you would like to share the family history you have preserved—share it with generations to come.

If you've answered the questions in *To Our Children's Children,* you know that stories beget stories, that one memory leads to another, allowing moments of life to be rekindled in your mind.

Just as the stories of your family prime the well of your own memory, they can help others tell their stories. Hearing other people's stories reminds us of happenings in our own lives. Before we know it we are traveling all the marvelous tangents of memory that lead us off from there.

If you have a favorite answer to one of the questions in *To Our Children's Children,* we'd love for you to share it with us. It can be the answer to any of the questions in the book—it can be a big one or a small one. It can be "Can you remember what you daydreamed about as you looked out of your bedroom window in the house of your growing up?" or "If you had all the time in the world, what would you do?" or "What is your favorite Campbell's soup?"

If you'd like to choose a story or two that you enjoyed telling while preserving your family history, we will try to gather a collection for a future volume. When you send us your stories, please make sure you send a copy that we can keep. Your stories will help others pass along their own.

You can mail your story to:

To Our Children's Children
P.O. Box 1086
Virginia City, Nevada 89440

Thanks. We look forward to hearing from you.

Bob Greene is a syndicated columnist for the *Chicago Tribune*. His column appears in more than two hundred newspapers in the United States, Canada and Japan. For nine years his "American Beat" was the lead column in *Esquire* magazine; as a broadcast journalist he has served as contributing correspondent for *ABC News Nightline*. In addition to *To Our Children's Children*, his national bestsellers include *Hang Time: Days and Dreams with Michael Jordan; Be True to Your School;* and *Good Morning, Merry Sunshine*.

D. G. Fulford is a freelance journalist and award-winning former columnist for the *Los Angeles Daily News* and the *New York Times* News Service.

Greene and Fulford are brother and sister.